AEROFILMS GUIDE

Football Grounds

Fully Revised 15th Edition For The 2007/2008 Season

D1477285

AEROFILMS GUIDE

Football Grounds

Fully Revised 15th Edition For The 2007/2008 Season

Every Barclaycard FA Premiership and Carling League Club

Ian Allan
PUBLISHING

Wembley

Wembley Stadium
Wembley National Stadium Ltd, Empire Way, Wembley, London HA9 0DS

Telephone: 020 8795 9000
Fax: 020 8795 5050
Web Site: www.wembleystadium.com
Brief History: Inaugurated for the FA Cup Final of 1923, venue for many national and international matches including the World Cup Final of 1966. Also traditionally used for other major sporting events and as a venue for rock concerts and other entertainments. Last used as a football ground for a World Cup qualifier against West Germany in October 2001. The original Wembley with its twin towers was demolished in 2002 when work started on the construction of the new ground. After some delay, the new Wembley was completed in the spring of 2007 with its first major match being the FA Cup Final in May 2007. Record attendance at original Wembley: 126,047; at rebuilt ground: 89,826
(Total) Current Capacity: 90,000 (all-seated)
Visiting Supporters' Allocation: not applicable
Nearest Railway Station: Wembley complex (Network Rail), Wembley Central (Network Rail and London Underground) and Wembley Park (London Underground)
Parking (Car): Very limited at the ground with residents' only schemes in adjacent housing areas.
Parking (Coach/Bus): As directed
Police Force: Metropolitan
Disabled Visitors' Facilities:
Wheelchairs: 310 spaces for wheelchair-bound fans throughout the ground
Blind: to be confirmed
Anticipated Development(s):

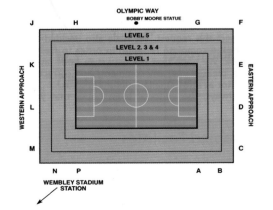

1 Olympic Way
2 Statue of Bobby Moore
3 To Wembley Park station
4 Wembley Complex railway station
5 To London Marylebone
6 To Wembley Central
7 Eastern Approach
8 Turnstiles 'G'
9 Turnstiles 'H'
10 Turnstiles 'F'
11 Turnstiles 'E'
12 Turnstiles 'D'

↘ North direction (approx)

◄ 700883
▼ 700884

Accrington Stanley

Fraser Eagle Stadium
Livingstone Road, Accrington, Lancashire BB5 5BX

Telephone: 01254 356950

Advance Tickets Tel No: 01254 356950

Fax: 01254 356951

Web Site: www.accringtonstanley.co.uk

E-mail: info@accringtonstanley.co.uk

League: League Two

Last Season: 20th
(P 46; W13; D 11; L 22; GF 70; GA 81)

Training Ground: New facility being sought for the 2007/08 season

Nickname: The Reds, Stanley

Nicknames: Stanley; The Reds

Brief History: The original club was formed as Accrington Villa in 1891 becoming Accrington Stanley in 1895. The team entered the Football League in 1921 and remained a member until its resignation in 1962. Following four years outside the League, the original club folded in 1966 and was not resurrected until 1970. The club has been based at the Crown Ground (now called the Fraser Eagle stadium) since it was reformed but prior to 1966 the original club played at Peel Park, which is now demolished. Record Attendance (at Fraser Eagle Stadium) 4,368

(Total) Current Capacity: 5,057 (1,200 seated)

Visiting Supporters' Allocation: 400-1,500 max (in Coppice Terrace — open)

Club Colours: Red shirts and white shorts

Nearest Railway Station: Accrington (20min walk)

Parking (Car): Free places at ground located behind both goals; on-street parking in vicinity of ground

Parking (Coach/Bus): As directed

Police Force and Tel No: Lancashire Police (01254 382141)

Disabled Visitors' Facilities:
Wheelchairs; Available
Blind: No special facility

Anticipated Development(s):

A difficult first season back in the Football League saw John Coleman's Stanley struggle to make an impact in League Two with relegation being a real possibility until virtually the end of the season. Indeed, had the Football League been more draconian in its reaction to Stanley's use of an ineligible player — he was only selected as a substitute and never actually played for the club — then a deduction of points and relegation might well have followed. One highpoint in an otherwise disappointing season was perhaps the home victory 1-0 over League One Nottingham Forest in the first round of the Carling Cup on 21 August. For the new season, it looks as though Stanley will face another battle to avoid the drop and perhaps safety for another year is possibly the best that the fans can look forward to.

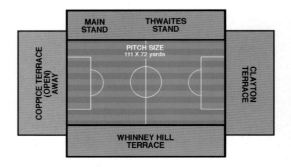

1 A680 Whalley Road
2 To town centre and
   Accrington BR station
   (one mile)
3 Livingstone Road
4 Cleveleys Road
5 Coppice Terrace (away)

N

➘ North direction (approx)

◄ 700440
▼ 700450

Arsenal

Emirates Stadium
Drayton Park, London N5 1BU

Telephone: 020 7704 4000

Advance Tickets Tel No: 020 7704 4040

Fax: 020 7704 4001

Web Site: www.arsenal.com

E-mail: info@arsenal.co.uk

League: F.A. Premier

Last Season: 4th
(P 38; W 19; D 11; L 8; GF 63; GA35)

Training Ground: Bell Lane, London Colney, St Albans AL2 1DR

Nickname: The Gunners

Brief History: Founded 1886 as Royal Arsenal, changed to Woolwich Arsenal in 1891 and Arsenal in 1914. Former grounds: Plumstead Common, Sportsman Ground, Manor Ground (twice), moved to Arsenal Stadium in 1913 and to new Emirates Stadium for start of the 2006/07 season. Record attendance (at Highbury) 73,295; 60,132 (at Emirates Stadium)

(Total) Current Capacity: 60,432

Visiting Supporters' Allocation: 3,000 (South East Corner)

Club Colours: Red and white shirts, white shorts

Nearest Railway Station: Finsbury Park or Drayton Park (Network Rail); Arsenal and Holloway Road (Underground)

Parking (Car): Residents' only parking scheme with special permits in the streets surrounding the ground and local road closures on matchdays

Parking (Coach/Bus): Queensland Road and Sobell Centre car park or as directed by the police

Police Force and Tel No: Metropolitan (020 7263 9090)

Disabled Visitors' Facilities:
Wheelchairs: c250 places around the ground
Blind: tbc

Anticipated Development(s): The club moved into the new Emirates Stadium for the start of the 2006/07 season, leaving Highbury, its home for the past 93 years, to be redeveloped as apartments although the work will incorporate the listed structures at the ground.

A strange season for the Gunners that started with all the promise of the new Emirates Stadium ended up with considerable uncertainty as one of the club's most influential directors, David Dein, resigned and as an American billionaire hovered with a view to joining the increasing number of owners from across the pond acquiring English clubs. Dein's departure again focused attention on the future of Arsene Wenger as manager and of star player Thierry Henry (who confirmed his departure for Barcelona for £16 million in late June). Although the likelihood is that Wenger will still be at the club in 2007/08 — Wenger has never broken a contract and his current deal expires at the end of the season — the uncertainty can't be helpful for a club that never really performed up to its own high standards in 2006/07. Whilst the Emirates Stadium has been something of a fortress for the team — only West Ham United proved victorious there (and that was after defending in a style reminiscent of the Alamo) — the Gunners proved to be suspect on their travels. Although never seriously challenging in the Premiership, a Champions League spot was again secured. In the cups, Arsenal failed to build on the Champions League Final of 2005/06 and the 2006/07 season will go down as one of some disappointment. With Wenger looking to overhaul his team in 2007/08, it's hard to escape the conclusion that 2007/08 will again see Arsenal out of the running for the title with one of the cup competitions offering the team's best chance for silverware.

Club Address: Highbury House, 75 Drayton Park, London N5 1BU

Best team in

Premier league

1 North Bridge
2 South Bridge
3 Drayton Park Station
4 Drayton Park
5 East Coast Main Line
6 To Finsbury Park Station
7 To Arsenal Underground Station
8 South East Corner (away)

↘ North direction (approx)

700919
700914

Villa Park
Trinity Road, Birmingham, B6 6HE

Tel No: 0871 423 8100

Advance Tickets Tel No: 0871 423 8101

Fax: 0871 423 8102

Web Site: www.avfc.premiumtv.co.uk

E-Mail: commercial.dept@astonvilla-fc.co.uk

League: F.A. Premier

Last Season: 11th
(P 38; W 11; D 17; L 10; GF 43; GA 41)

Training Ground: Bodymoor Heath Lane, Middleton, Tamworth B78 2BB

Nickname: The Villans

Brief History: Founded in 1874. Founder Members Football League (1888). Former Grounds: Aston Park and Lower Aston Grounds and Perry Barr, moved to Villa Park (a development of the Lower Aston Grounds) in 1897. Record attendance 76,588

(Total) Current Capacity: 42,573 (all seated)

Visiting Supporters' Allocation: Approx 2,983 in North Stand

Club Colours: Claret and blue shirts, white shorts

Nearest Railway Station: Witton

Parking (Car): Asda car park, Aston Hall Road

Parking (Coach/Bus): Asda car park, Aston Hall Road (special coach park for visiting supporters situated in Witton Lane)

Police Force and Tel No: West Midlands (0121 322 6010)

Disabled Visitors' Facilities:
Wheelchairs: Trinity Road Stand section
Blind: Commentary by arrangement

Anticipated Development(s): In order to increase the ground's capacity to 51,000 Planning Permission has been obtained to extend the North Stand with two corner in-fills. There is, however, no confirmed timescale for the work to be completed.

One of a number of clubs to change hands during the course of the season, Aston Villa were acquired by the American tycoon Randy Lerner in the autumn, ending the reign of Doug Ellis after many years. On the field, Martin O'Neill's team improved their position considerably over that achieved the previous year, proving themselves one of the harder team to beat in the division, although drawing too many games seriously to challenge for a UEFA Cup spot. With the owner's backing, O'Neill should be able to make some significant signings for the 2007/08 season and a realistic challenge for a UEFA Cup spot should certainly be within the team's capabilities. As with the other Premier League teams outside the top three or four, the club's best opportunity for silverware is most likely to come from one of the cup competitions.

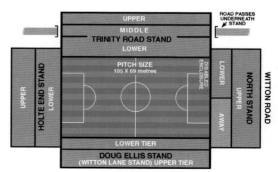

C Club Offices
S Club Shop
E Entrance(s) for visiting supporters
R Refreshment bars for visiting supporters
T Toilets for visiting supporters

1 B4137 Witton Lane
2 B4140 Witton Road
3 Trinity Road
4 To A4040 Aston Lane to A34 Walsall Road
5 To Aston Expressway & M6
6 Holte End
7 Visitors' Car Park
8 Witton railway station
9 North Stand
10 Trinity Road Stand

↘ North direction (approx)

◄ 697435
▼ 697425

Barnet

Underhill Stadium
Barnet Lane, Barnet, Herts EN5 2DN

Telephone: 020 8441 6932

Advance Tickets Tel No: 020 8449 6325

Fax: 020 8447 0655

Web site: www.barnetfc.premiumtv.co.uk

E-mail: info@barnetfc.com

League: League Two

Last Season: 15th
(P 46; W 16; D 11; L 19; GF 55; GA 70)

Nickname: The Bees

Brief History: Founded 1888 as Barnet Alston. Changed name to Barnet (1919). Former grounds: Queens Road and Totteridge Lane; moved to Underhill in 1906. Promoted to Football League 1991; relegated to Conference 2001; promoted to League 2 2005. Record attendance, 11,026

(Total) Current Capacity: 5,500

Visiting Supporters' Allocation: 1,000 on South Stand (open) plus 500 on East Terrace is required.

Colours: Black and gold shirts, black shorts

Nearest Railway Station: New Barnet (High Barnet — Tube)

Parking (Car): Street Parking and High Barnet station

Parking (Coach/Bus): As directed by police

Police Force and Tel No: Metropolitan (020 8200 2112)

Disabled Visitors' Facilities:
Wheelchairs: 12 positions on east side of North Terrace
Blind: No special facility

Anticipated Development(s): The club's long-term ambition remains to relocate from Underhill and announced that, in the event of being unable to locate a suitable site within the borough, it would look outside Barnet provided that any new site was within a 'reasonable travelling distance' of the existing ground. The former has proved difficult as availability of a suitable site within the borough is limited and, in late June 2007, it was announced that the club would seek to rebuild Underhill in order to provide the 2,000 covered seats if the club was to retain its League status at the end of the 2007/08 season. The £7 million scheme envisages the purchase of some surrounding property and the construction of two new stands at either end of the ground. However, the club sees this redevelopment as an interim measure whilst it continues its search for a new ground.

Although at one stage it looked as though Paul Fairclough's team might have got dragged into the relegation battle, a late run saw the team achieve a position of mid-table safety, albeit with only six points more than that achieved when finishing 18th at the end of 2005/06. Although the club did score more goals in 2006/07 than in the previous season, the number conceded — 70 — was amongst the highest in the division and this defensive frailty will need to be addressed during the close season if the Bees aren't going to resume their annual flirtation with the drop. Away from the league, one high point was the 2-0 victory away at Championship high-fliers Cardiff City in the first round of the Carling Cup in August 2006. For 2007/08, the Bees can look forward to two new London-based teams and probably a bottom half finish. The team should be too good to face a relegation battle but a further season of consolidation is perhaps the best that the Underhill faithful can look forward to.

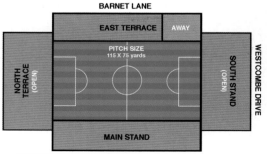

C Club Offices
S Club Shop
E Entrance(s) for visiting supporters
R Refreshment bars for visiting supporters
T Toilets for visiting supporters

1 Barnet Lane
2 Westcombe Drive
3 A1000 Barnet Hill
4 New Barnet BR station (one mile)
5 To High Barnet tube station, M1 and M25
6 South Terrace

↘ North direction (approx)

◄ 699356
▼ 699359

Barnsley

Oakwell Stadium
Grove Street, Barnsley, S71 1ET

Tel No: 01226 211211

Advance Tickets Tel No: 01226 211200

Fax: 01226 211444

Web Site: www.barnsleyfc.premiumtv.co.uk

E-mail: marketing@barnsleyfc.co.uk

League: League Championship

Last Season: 20th
(P 46; W 15; D 5; L 26; GF 53; GA 85)

Training Ground: Adjacent to ground

Nickname: The Tykes

Brief History: Founded in 1887 as Barnsley St Peter's, changed name to Barnsley in 1897. Former Ground: Doncaster Road, Worsboro Bridge until 1888. Record attendance 40,255

(Total) Current Capacity: 23,009 (all seated)

Visiting Supporters' Allocation: 6,000 maximum (all seated; North Stand)

Club Colours: Red shirts, white shorts

Nearest Railway Station: Barnsley

Parking (Car): Queen's Ground car park

Parking (Coach/Bus): Queen's Ground car park

Police Force and Tel No: South Yorkshire (01266 206161)

Disabled Visitors' Facilities:
Wheelchairs: Purpose built disabled stand
Blind: Commentary available

Future Development(s): With the completion of the new North Stand with its 6,000 capacity, the next phase for the redevelopment of Oakwell will feature the old West Stand with its remaining open seating. There is, however, no timescale for this work.

Despite having guided the Tykes to the League Championship at the end of 2005/06, a poor start to the season, which left the team struggling in the relegation zone, cost Andy Ritchie his job at the end of November. He was replaced as caretaker by Simon Davey, who, after a run of games took the club out of the drop zone, was confirmed in the position full-time at the end of December. Under Davey the club's position improved although it was not until towards the end of the campaign that the team's League Championship status was assured. This was probably just as well, as the team's final match of the season resulted in a 7-0 drubbing by Play-Off chasing West Brom. The result epitomised Barnsley's problem: the club had the worst defensive record in the Championship and, apart from relegated Southend, the worst goal difference. It's hard to escape the conclusion that Barnsley will have a further struggle to avoid the drop in 2007/08 unless these defensive frailties can be sorted out

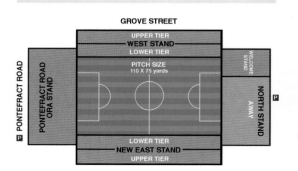

C Club Offices
S Club Shop
E Entrance(s) for visiting supporters

1 A628 Pontefract Road
2 To Barnsley Exchange BR station and M1 Junction 37 (two miles)
3 Queen's Ground Car Park
4 North Stand
5 Grove Street
6 To Town Centre

↘ North direction (approx)

◄ 697496
▼ 697497

Birmingham City

St Andrew's Stadium
St Andrew's Street, Birmingham, B9 4NH

Tel No: 0871 226 1875

Advance Tickets Tel No: 0871 226 1875

Fax: 0121 766 7866

Web Site: www.bcfc.premiumtv.co.uk

E-Mail: reception@bcfc.com

League: F.A. Premiership

Last Season: 2nd (promoted)
(P 46; W 26; D 8; L 12; GF 67; GA 49)

Training Ground: Wasts Hall, Redhill Road, Kings Norton, Birmingham B38 9EJ. 0121 244 1401

Nickname: The Blues

Brief History: Founded 1875, as Small Heath Alliance. Changed to Small Heath in 1888, Birmingham in 1905, Birmingham City in 1945. Former Grounds: Arthur Street, Ladypool Road, Muntz Street, moved to St Andrew's in 1906. Record attendance 66,844

(Total) Current Capacity: 30,016 (all seated)

Visiting Supporters' Allocation: 3-4,500 in new Railway End (Lower Tier)

Club Colours: Blue and white shirts, white shorts

Nearest Railway Station: Bordesley

Parking (Car): Street parking

Parking (Coach/Bus): Coventry Road

Police Force and Tel No: West Midlands (0121 772 1169)

Disabled Visitors' Facilities:
Wheelchairs: 90 places; advanced notice required
Blind: Commentary available

Future Development(s): The proposals for the Digbeth ground have not progressed and any future development is likely to involve work at St Andrews, where there are plans for the possible redevelopment of the Main Stand to take the ground's capacity to 36,500. There is no timescale for the £12 million project and with the club's relegation from the Premier League every possibility that it will be deferred.

Relegated at the end of 2005/06, much was expected of Steve Bruce's team and, in getting promotion back to the Premier League at the first time of asking, the Blues certainly delivered. However, it wasn't quite the easy progression that it seemed with strong competition from both Derby County and from the eventual champions Sunderland. Away from the league, City achieved one of the more remarkable cup victories of the season, when the team defeated Newcastle United 5-1 in the third round match at St James's Park — a result that did not go down well with the Toon faithful. For 2006/07, Bruce was in the fortunate position that he'd managed to retain the core of the team that had come down from the Premier League; if, however, the Blues are to make a decent fist of retaining their Premier League come May 2008, the squad will need to be considerably strengthened. It's hard to escape the conclusion that the St Andrews faithful can look forward to a long winter battling against the drop.

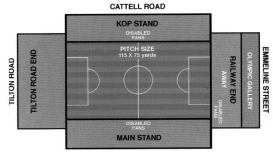

C Club Offices
S Club Shop
E Entrance(s) for visiting
   supporters

1 Car Park
2 B4128 Cattell Road
3 Tilton Road
4 Garrison Lane
5 To A4540 & A38 (M)
6 To City Centre and
   New Street BR Station
   (1½ miles)
7 Railway End
8 Tilton Road End
9 Main Stand
10 Kop Stand
11 Emmeline Street
12 Kingston Road
13 St Andrew's Street

↘ North direction (approx)

◀ 699252
▼ 699246

Ewood Park
Blackburn, Lancashire, BB2 4JF

Tel No: 08701 113232

Advance Tickets Tel No: 08701 123456

Fax: 01254 671042

Web Site: www.rovers.premiumtv.co.uk

E-Mail: commercial@rovers.co.uk

League: FA Premier

Last Season: 11th (P 38; W 15; D 7; L 16; GF 52; GA 54)

Training Ground: Brockhall Training Ground, The Avenue, Brockhall Village, Blackburn BB6 8AW

Nickname: Rovers

Brief History: Founded 1875. Former Grounds: Oozebooth, Pleasington Cricket Ground, Alexandra Meadows. Moved to Ewood Park in 1890. Founder members of Football League (1888). Record attendance 61,783

(Total) Current Capacity: 31,367 (all seated)

Visiting Supporters' Allocation: 3,914 at the Darwen End

Club Colours: Blue and white halved shirts, white shorts

Nearest Railway Station: Blackburn

Parking (Car): Street parking and c800 spaces at ground

Parking (Coach/Bus): As directed by Police

Police Force and Tel No: Lancashire (01254 51212)

Disabled Visitors' Facilities:
Wheelchairs: All sides of the ground
Blind: Commentary available

Anticipated Development(s): There remain plans to redevelop the Riverside (Walker Steel) Stand to take Ewood Park's capacity to c40,000, but there is no confirmation as to if and when this work will be undertaken.

Having experienced European football in 2006/07, finishing in 11th position — as opposed to 6th the previous year — might be regarded as a disappointing conclusion to the campaign but Rovers is one of those middling Premier League teams where a couple of results can make the difference between a top half or bottom half finish. Ultimately, the success of a club like Rovers comes down to money — and the fact that during the close season Rovers was one of a number of Premier League teams to fall into foreign ownership means that Mark Hughes may well have additional funding to strengthen his squad. The downside, however, is that other middle ranking teams are likely to be in the same position. Moreover as the level of funding for these clubs increases so too do the costs of acquisition of and players' salaries. There's an awful lot of running hard to stand still going on with Premier League teams and, if the deal goes through, Rovers could find that their massive potential investment will lead only again to a high mid-table position come May 2008.

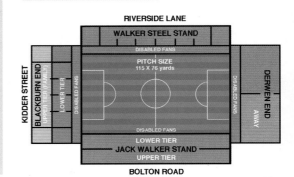

C Club Offices
S Club Shop
E Entrance(s) for visiting supporters
R Refreshment bars for visiting supporters
T Toilets for visiting supporters

1 A666 Bolton Road
2 Kidder Street
3 Nuttall Street
4 Town Centre & Blackburn Central BR station (1½ miles)
5 To Darwen and Bolton
6 Darwen End
7 Car Parks
8 Top O'Croft Road

➘ North direction (approx)

◂ 698991
▾ 698999

Blackpool

Seasiders Way
Blackpool, Lancashire, FY1 6JJ

Tel No: 0870 443 1953

Advance Tickets Tel No: 0870 443 1953

Fax: 01253 405011

E-Mail: info@blackpoolfc.co.uk

Web Site: www.blackpoolfcpremiumtv.co.uk

League: League Championship

Last Season: 3rd (promoted)
(P 46; W 24; D 11; L 11; GF 76; GA 64)

Training Ground: Squires Gate Training Ground,
Martin Avenue, Lytham St Annes FY8 2SJ

Nickname: The Seasiders

Brief History: Founded 1887, merged with
'South Shore' (1899). Former grounds: Raikes
Hall (twice) and Athletic Grounds, Stanley
Park, South Shore played at Cow Cap Lane,
moved to Bloomfield Road in 1899. Record
attendance 38,098

(Total) Current Capacity: 9,491 (all seated)

Visiting Supporters' Allocation: 1,700 (all
seated) in East Stand (open)

Club Colours: Tangerine shirts, white shorts

Nearest Railway Station: Blackpool South

Parking (Car): At Ground and street parking
(also behind West Stand – from M55)

Parking (Coach/Bus): Mecca car park (behind
North End (also behind West Stand – from
M55)

Other Club Sharing Ground: Blackpool
Panthers RLFC

Police Force and Tel No: Lancashire (01253
293933)

Disabled Visitors' Facilities:
Wheelchairs: North and West stands
Blind: Commentary available (limited
numbers)

Anticipated Development(s): The go-ahead has
been given to the construction of the new
South Stand, although whether this is a
temporary structure (similar to that already
erected on the east of the ground) or a
permanent structure has yet to be
determined. It is hoped to have the facility
available for the start of the 2007/08 season
— although too late to be recorded in the
photographs — and this will raise the
ground's capacity to 13,000. It is likely that
any new structure will initially lack a roof.

Having survived in League One — just — at the end
of the 2005/06 season, Blackpool was taken over
by the Latvian businessman Valeri Belokon, who
promised to invest some £5 million in the Seasiders.
Under Simon Grayson, and with the backing of
Belokon, the club did made significant progress during
the 2006/07 season and right up to the end of the
campaign the team was in with a shout of automatic
promotion. Indeed, if results had gone Blackpool's way
during the final Saturday it would have been
Blackpool rather than Bristol City promoted alongside
Scunthorpe. However, despite a 6-3 victory away at
Swansea City, Bristol's 3-1 defeat of relegated
Rotherham consigned Blackpool to the Play-Offs and a
semi-final against Oldham. Victory over the two legs
took Blackpool to Wembley for a final against Yeovil
Town. Victory over the Somerset team brings second-
tier football to Blackpool for the first time in some
three decades. As with all promoted teams,
Blackpool's first task will be to consolidate itself at the
higher level but — with the example of Colchester
United to follow — there is every possibility that
Blackpool could have some success in the
Championship, particularly if Grayson continues to get
the backing of Belokon for further investment in the
squad.

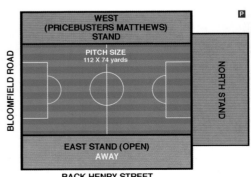

1 Car Park
2 To Blackpool South BR Station (1½ miles) and M55 Junction 4
3 Bloomfield Road
4 Central Drive
5 Henry Street
6 East Stand (away)
7 Site of South Stand
8 West (Pricebusters Matthews) Stand
9 North Stand

N

↘ North direction (approx)

◄ 700486
▼ 700490

Bolton Wanderers

Reebok Stadium
Burnden Way, Lostock, Bolton, BL6 6JW

Tel No: 01204 673673

Advance Tickets Tel No: 0871 871 2932

Fax: 01204 673773

E-Mail: reception@bwfc.co.uk

Web Site: www.bwfc.premiumtv.co.uk

League: FA Premier

Last Season: 7th
(P 38; W 16; D 8; L 14; GF 47; GA 52)

Training Ground: Euxton Training Ground, Euxton Lane, Chorley PR7 6FA

Nickname: The Trotters

Brief History: Founded 1874 as Christ Church; name changed 1877. Former grounds: Several Fields, Pikes Lane (1880-95) and Burnden Park (1895-1997). Moved to Reebok Stadium for 1997/98 season. Record attendance (Burnden Park): 69,912. Record attendance of 28,353 at Reebok Stadium

(Total) Current Capacity: 28,723 (all-seater)

Visiting Supporters' Allocation: 5,200 maximum (South Stand)

Club Colours: White shirts, white shorts

Nearest Railway Station: Horwich Parkway

Parking (Car): 2,800 places at ground with up 3,000 others in proximity

Parking (Coach/Bus): As directed

Police Force and Tel No: Greater Manchester (01204 522466)

Disabled Visitors' Facilities:
Wheelchairs: c100 places around the ground
Blind: Commentary available

Anticipated Developments(s): The station at Horwich Parkway has now opened. There are currently no further plans for the development of the Reebok Stadium.

Although 2006/07 will go down as another successful season at the Reebok, there is definitely a feeling that an era has ended with the replacement of 'Big Sam' with erstwhile assistant 'Little Sam'. On the pitch, Wanderers ultimately finished in seventh place, thus guaranteeing the team a place in the UEFA Cup for 2007/08, but this triumph was overshadowed earlier in the season by the Panorama broadcast linking Sam Allardyce to transfer irregularities — accusations which he has strenuously denied — and, shortly before the end of the season, with Allardyce's resignation. The club moved quickly to appoint Sammy Lee as the new manager but Lee will have his work cut out if he going to match Allardyce's ability both to attract the star players to Bolton and also to draw performances out from them. Allardyce's triumph was to convert Bolton from being a yo-yo club to one with Premier League staying power. The fear for Wanderers' fans is that Allardyce's squad will break up and that it will be difficult to bring in new players. Figures like Anelka may well not be around at the start of the new season and, without investing in new talent, Bolton could be one of the dark horses for a struggle against the drop

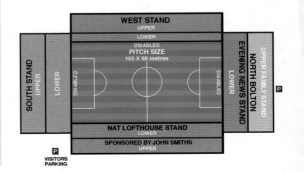

1 To Junction 6 of M61
2 A6027 Horwich link road
3 South Stand (away)
4 North Stand
5 Nat Lofthouse Stand
6 West Stand
7 M61 northbound to M6 and Preston (at J6)
8 M61 southbound to Manchester (at J6)
9 To Horwich and Bolton
10 To Lostock Junction BR station
11 To Horwich Parkway station

North direction (approx)

◀ 699055
▾ 699053

25

Bournemouth

The Fitness First Stadium
Dean Court, Bournemouth, Dorset, BH7 7AF

Tel No: 01202 726300

Advance Tickets Tel No: 0845 330 1000; 08700 340380

Fax: 01202 726301

E-Mail: enquiries@afcb.co.uk

Web Site: www.afcb.premiumtv.co.uk

League: League One

Last Season: 19th (P46; W 13; D 13; L 20; GF 50; GA 64)

Training Ground: Canford School, Court House, Canford Magna, Wimborne BH21 3AF

Nickname: The Cherries

Brief History: Founded 1890 as Boscombe St. John's, changed to Boscombe (1899), Bournemouth & Boscombe Athletic (1923) and A.F.C. Bournemouth (1971). Former grounds Kings Park (twice) and Castlemain Road, Pokesdown. Moved to Dean Court in 1910. Record attendance 28,799; since rebuilding: 9,359

(Total) Current Capacity: 10,700 (all seated)

Visiting Supporters' Allocation: 1,500 in East Stand (can be increased to 2,000 if required)

Club Colours: Red and black shirts, black shorts

Nearest Railway Station: Bournemouth

Parking (Car): Large car park adjacent ground

Parking (Coach/Bus): Large car park adjacent ground

Police Force and Tel No: Dorset (01202 552099)

Disabled Visitors' Facilities:
Wheelchairs: 100 spaces
Blind: No special facility

Anticipated Development(s): The club still intends to construct a South Stand at Dean Court, taking the ground's capacity to just under 12,000 but there is no confirmed schedule.

In early September, after spending 23 years with the club in various roles, and latterly as manager, Sean O'Driscoll announced his departure to take over as boss at Doncaster Rovers. Youth team coach Joe Roach and goalkeeping coach Stuart Murdoch were handed temporary charge for the game against Crewe (which the Cherries won 1-0). In mid-October it was announced that Kevin Bond had been appointed to the post full-time. Under Bond, the Cherries faced a battle to retain the club's League One status, although the team's survival was assured — just — before a last-day defeat at Port Vale. Away from the league, Bournemouth suffered a home defeat by League Two outfit Bristol Rovers in an FA Cup second round replay at Dean Court. With the four teams being promoted from League Two — including Bristol Rovers — looking potentially much stronger than the quartet that was relegated, it looks as though Bournemouth may well have a long struggle ahead to ensure League One survival in 2007/08.

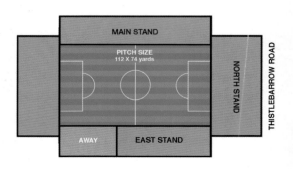

Club Offices

1 Car Park
2 A338 Wessex Way
3 To Bournemouth BR Station (1½ miles)
4 To A31 & M27
5 Thistlebarrow Road
6 King's Park Drive
7 Littledown Avenue
8 North Stand
9 Main Stand
10 East Stand
11 Site of proposed South Stand

N

↘ North direction (approx)

◄ 700388
▼ 700382

Bradford City

Intersonic Stadium
Valley Parade, Bradford, BD8 7DY

Tel No: 0870 822 0000

Advance Tickets Tel No: 0870 822 1911

Fax: 01274 773356

Web Site: www.bradfordcityfc.premiumtv.co.uk

E-Mail: bradfordcityfc@compuserve.com

League: League Two

Last Season: 22nd (relegated) (P 46; W 11; D 14; L 21; GF 47; GA 65)

Training Ground: Rawdon Meadows, Apperley Bridge, Bradford

Nickname: The Bantams

Brief History: Founded 1903 (formerly Manningham Northern Union Rugby Club founded in 1876). Continued use of Valley Parade, joined 2nd Division on re-formation. Record attendance: 39,146

(Total) Current Capacity: 25,136 (all seated)

Visiting Supporters' Allocation: 1,130 (all seated) in TL Dallas stand plus seats in Midland Road Stand if required

Club Colours: Claret and amber shirts, claret shorts

Nearest Railway Station: Bradford Forster Square

Parking (Car): Street parking and car parks

Parking (Coach/Bus): As directed by Police

Police Force and Tel No: West Yorkshire (01274 723422)

Disabled Visitors' Facilities:
Wheelchairs: 110 places in Sunwin, CIBA and Carlsberg stands
Blind: Commentary available

Anticipated Development(s): With work on the Main (Sunwin) Stand now completed, Valley Parade has a slightly imbalanced look. The club has proposals for the reconstruction of the Midland Road (Yorkshire First) Stand to take the ground's capacity to 30,000, although, given the club's current financial position, there is no time-scale.

A promising start to the season, when the Bantams seemed to be making a decent push towards the Play-Offs, seen petered out and, with the team gradually drifting down the League One table, the decision to sack Colin Todd in mid-February, following a 1-0 reverse at Gillingham that left the team three points above the drop zone, came as little surprise to the regulars at Valley Parade. Todd, who had been in the position for almost three years and had guided the team through its recent financial troubles, was replaced on a caretaker basis by team captain David Wetherall who celebrated confirmation that he'd retain the position until the end of the season by notching up his first win — a 3-2 triumph at promotion chasing Bristol City. However, it was a short term respite, as the team's form — particularly at home (where defeat against fellow strugglers Leyton Orient was critical) — consigned the Bantams to League Two. Shortly after the end of the season it was confirmed that City legend Stuart McCall would take over as boss for the 2007/08 season. He — and the fans — will take heart from the fact that the three teams automatically promoted at the end of 2006/07 had been relegated at the end of the previous season. City should be one of the pacemakers in 2007/08 and should achieve a Play-Off place at worst.

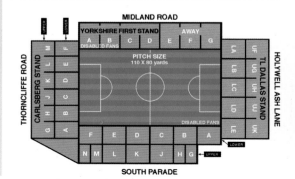

C Club Offices
S Club Shop
E Entrance(s) for visiting supporters
R Refreshment bars for visiting supporters
T Toilets for visiting supporters

1 Midland Road
2 Valley Parade
3 A650 Manningham Lane
4 To City Centre, Forster Square and Interchange BR Stations M606 & M62
5 To Keighley
6 Car Parks
7 Sunwin Stand
8 Midland (Yorkshire First) Stand
9 TL Dallas Stand
10 Carlsberg Stand

↘ North direction (approx)

◄ 700121
▼ 700114

Griffin Park
Braemar Road, Brentford, Middlesex, TW8 0NT

Tel No: 0845 3456 442

Advance Tickets Tel No: 0845 3456 442

Fax: 020 8380 9937

Web Site: www.brentfordfc.premiumtv.co.uk

E-Mail: enquiries@brentfordfc.co.uk

League: League Two

Last Season: 24th (relegated)
(P46; W 8; D 13; L 25; GF 40; GA 79)

Training Ground: Osterley Training Ground, 100 Jersey Road, Hounslow TW5 0TP

Nickname: The Bees

Brief History: Founded 1889. Former Grounds: Clifden House Ground, Benn's Field (Little Ealing), Shotters Field, Cross Roads, Boston Park Cricket Ground, moved to Griffin Park in 1904. Founder-members Third Division (1920). Record attendance 38,678

(Total) Current Capacity: 12,763 (8,905 seated)

Visiting Supporters' Allocation: 1,600 in Brook Road Stand (600 seated)

Club Colours: Red and white striped shirts, black shorts

Nearest Railway Station: Brentford, South Ealing (tube)

Parking (Car): Street parking (restricted)

Parking (Coach/Bus): Layton Road car park

Other Club Sharing Ground: Chelsea Reserves

Police Force and Tel No: Metropolitan (020 8577 1212)

Disabled Visitors' Facilities:
Wheelchairs: Braemar Road
Blind: Commentary available

Anticipated Development(s): Although the club's long-term intention is to relocate, in mid-December 2004 it was announced that the Football Foundation would grant the club £1,775,950 for work at Griffin Park, provided that plans were approved at a public meeting. Planned work includes modification of the New Road Stand and the provision of a roof over the Ealing Road Terrace. Although the original application was rejected by the planning authorities in December 2005, following local consultation plans were approved in mid-April 2006. The work will ultimately result in a capacity of 15,000 at Griffin Park.

A bright start to the season was soon followed by a rapid descent down the League One table, with the team failing to win on any of the previous 16 occasions, resulted in Leroy Rosenior being sacked as manager in mid-November after a 4-0 home defeat by Crewe that left the Bees deep in the League One drop zone. Scott Fitzgerald, the Youth Team coach, was immediately appointed caretaker as the club sought a permanent replacement. Unfortunately, Fitzgerald was unable to prevent the club's drift into League Tow and, after relegation was confirmed on Easter Monday following the defeat at Crewe, Fitzgerald resigned. Barry Quinn took over as caretaker. In late April, the club announced that Terry Butcher had been appointed boss from the start of the 2007/08 season. As with the other teams relegated from League One at the end of 2006/07, Butcher will be hoping that the precedent set by three of the teams relegated at the end of 2005/06 being promoted automatically will hold firm for the 2007/08 campaign. The Bees should be one of those teams pushing for promotion and the Play-Offs.

C Club Offices
S Club Shop
E Entrance(s) for visiting
    supporters

1 Ealing Road
2 Braemar Road
3 Brook Road South
4 To M4 (¼ mile) & South
    Ealing Tube Station
    (1 mile)
5 Brentford BR Station
6 To A315 High Street &
    Kew Bridge
7 New Road
8 Ealing Road Terrace
9 Brook Road Stand (away)

↘ North direction (approx)

◄ 700195
▼ 700193

Withdean Stadium
Tongdean Lane, Brighton BN1 5JD

Tel No: 01273 695400
Fax: 01273 648179
Advance Ticket Tel No: 01273 776992
Web Site: www.seagulls.premiumtv.co.uk
E-Mail: seagulls@bhafc.co.uk
League: League Championship
Last Season: 18th (P46; W 14; D 11; L 21; GF 49; GA 58)
Training Ground: University of Sussex, Falmer Sports Complex, Ridge Road, Falmer, Brighton BN1 9PL
Nickname: The Seagulls
Brief History: Founded 1900 as Brighton & Hove Rangers, changed to Brighton & Hove Albion 1902. Former grounds: Home Farm (Withdean), County Ground, Goldstone Ground (1902-1997), Priestfield Stadium (ground share with Gillingham) 1997-1999; moved to Withdean Stadium 1999. Founder members of the 3rd Division 1920. Record attendance (at Goldstone Ground): 36,747; at Withdean Stadium: 7,999.
(Total) Current Capacity: 8,850 (all seated)
Visiting Supporters' Allocation: 900 max on open West Stand
Club Colours: Blue and white striped shirts, white shorts
Nearest Railway Station: Preston Park
Parking (Cars): Street parking in the immediate vicinity of the ground is residents' only. This will be strictly enforced and it is suggested that intending visitors should use parking facilities away from the ground and use the proposed park and ride bus services that will be provided.
Parking (Coach/Bus): As directed
Police Force and Tel No: Sussex (01273 778922)
Disabled Visitors' Facilities
Wheelchairs: Facilities in both North and South stands
Blind: No special facility
Anticipated Development(s): After a four-year campaign, permission for the construction of the new ground at Falmer was given by John Prescott at the end of October 2005. It was planned that work on the 23,000-seat capacity ground will start during 2006 with the intention of completion for the start of the 2007/08 season. However, Lewes District Council launched a legal challenge to the construction of the new ground and, in early March 2006, it was announced that this challenge would result in the ground being delayed with a new anticipated completion date of August 2009. A further development, on 6 April 2006, resulted in the original approval being quashed as a result of a mistake made in John Prescott's original letter of approval with the result that the matter would again have to be referred to him. In early July 2007 it was announced that £5.3 million had been awarded towards the cost of the construction of the ground from the South East England Development Agency provided that planning consent was given. Following the cabinet reshuffle, Hazel Blears gave the project the go-ahead at the end of July.

Following a disappointing start to the season, which left the Seagulls in 17th place following relegation at the end of the 2005/06 season, Mark McGhee was sacked as manager in early September after almost three years in the Withdean hot-seat. He was replaced, on a caretaker basis, by Dean Wilkins, the youth team coach, who was subsequently confirmed in the position on a permanent basis. Under Wilkins, the Seagulls survived in League One, ultimately finishing in 18th position. However, with the teams being promoted from League Two looking to have greater strength than the teams they replaced, it looks as though it's going to be another hard season at the Withdean Stadium if the club's League One status is going to be retained.

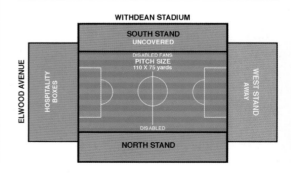

Shop Address:
6 Queen's Road, Brighton
Note: All games at Withdean will be
all-ticket with no cash
admissions on the day.

1 Withdean Stadium
2 London-Brighton railway line
3 To London Road (A23)
4 Tongdean Lane
5 Valley Drive
6 To Brighton town centre and main
   railway station (1.75 miles)
7 Tongdean Lane (with bridge under
   railway)
8 South Stand
9 A23 northwards to Crawley
10 To Preston Park railway station
11 North Stand
12 North East Stand
13 West Stand (away)

↘ North direction (approx)

◄ 699849
▼ 699861

Ashton Gate Stadium
Ashton Road, Bristol BS3 2EJ

Tel No: 0117 963 0630

Advance Tickets Tel No: 0870 112 1897

Fax: 0117 963 0700

Web Site: www.bcfc.premiumtv.co.uk

E-Mail: sales@bcfc.co.uk

League: League Championship

Last Season: 2nd (promoted)
(P 46; W 25; D 10; L 11; GF 63; GA 39)

Training Ground: Abbots Leigh, Abbots Leigh Road, Bristol BS8 3QD

Nickname: The Robins

Brief History: Founded 1894 as Bristol South End changed to Bristol City in 1897. Former Ground: St John's Lane, Bedminster, moved to Ashton Gate in 1904. Record attendance 43,335

(Total) Current Capacity: 21,479 prior to redevelopment (all seated)

Visiting Supporters' Allocation: 3,000 in Wedlock End (all seated; can be increased to 5,500 if necessary)

Club Colours: Red shirts, white shorts

Nearest Railway Station: Bristol Temple Meads

Parking (Car): Street parking

Parking (Coach/Bus): Marsh Road

Police Force and Tel No: Avon/Somerset (0117 927 7777)

Disabled Visitors' Facilities:
Wheelchairs: Limited
Blind: Commentary available

Anticipated Development(s): In February 2005 the club announced ambitious plans for the redevelopment of Ashton Gate with the intention of creating a 30,000 all-seated stadium. The first phase of the work, the replacement of the East (Wedlock) Stand with a new £7 million structure, was due to have started in 2005. However, delays mean work is now likely to take place after the end of the 2007/08 season. Whilst the work is in progress, the ground's capacity will be reduced to 15,000 and on completion, the overall capacity will be increased to 21,000. Once work on the East Stand is completed, the club's attentions will turn to the Williams and Donman stands.

After just missing out on the Play-Offs at the end of 2005/06, when a late burst of form took Gary Johnson's team rapidly up the League One table, there were expectations that the Robins would mount a serious challenge for promotion in 2006/07 and, in this, the team didn't disappoint. For much of the season automatic promotion seemed to be a three-horse race with Scunthorpe United, Nottingham Forest and City all involved but as the season progressed a fourth contender — Blackpool — also emerged and, on the final Saturday of the season, Forest, Blackpool or City could each have claimed the second automatic spot behind Scunthorpe. Despite Blackpool's victory and Forest's draw, City's 3-1 home victory over relegated Rotherham ensures League Championship football for Gary Johnson's team in 2007/08. As with other promoted teams, the first priority will be to ensure survival at this level, but City should have the potential to ensure that Championship status is assured.

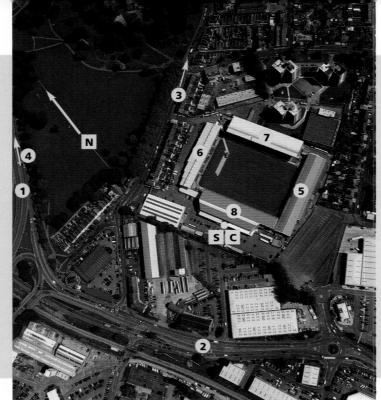

C Club Offices
S Club Shop

1 A370 Ashton Road
2 A3209 Winterstoke Road
3 To Temple Meads Station
  (1½ miles)
4 To City Centre, A4, M32 &
  M4
5 Database Wedlock Stand
  (prior to redevelopment)
6 Atyeo Stand
7 Brunel Ford Williams
  Stand
8 Dolman Stand

↘ North direction (approx)

◄ 699164
▾ 699177

Bristol Rovers

The Memorial Stadium
Filton Avenue, Horfield, Bristol BS7 0BF

Tel No: 0117 909 6648

Advance Tickets Tel No: 0117 909 6648

Fax: 0117 907 4312

Web Site: www.bristolrovers.premiumtv.co.uk

E-Mail: feedback@bristolrovers.co.uk

League: League One

Last Season: 6th (promoted)
(P46; W 20; D 12; L 14; GF 49; GA 42)

Training Ground: Bristol Academy of Sport, Filton College, Filton Avenue, Bristol BS34 7AT

Nickname: The Pirates (or Gasheads historically)

Brief History: Founded 1883 as Black Arabs, changed to Eastville Rovers (1884), Bristol Eastville Rovers (1896) and Bristol Rovers (1897). Former grounds: Purdown, Three Acres, The Downs (Horfield), Ridgeway, Bristol Stadium (Eastville), Twerton Park (1986-96), moved to The Memorial Ground 1996. Record attendance: (Eastville) 38,472, (Twerton Park) 9,813, (Memorial Ground) 11,433

(Total) Current Capacity: 11,917 (4,000 seated); standing capacity of 8,000 includes 500 on the Family Terrace

Visiting Supporters' Allocation: 1,132 (Centenary Stand Terrace; open)

Club Colours: Blue and white quartered shirts, white shorts

Nearest Railway Station: Filton or Stapleton Road

Parking (Car): Limited parking at ground for home fans only; street parking also available

Parking (Coach/Bus): As directed

Police Force and Tel No: Avon/Somerset (0117 927 7777)

Other Clubs Sharing Ground: Bristol Shoguns RUFC

Disabled Visitors' Facilities:
Wheelchairs: 35 wheelchair positions
Blind: Limited provision

Anticipated Development(s): It was announced in early June that work would commence on the redevelopment of the Memorial Stadium in early 2008 and that completion of the new 18,500 all-seater stadium would take some 18 months. During the second half of the 2007/08 season, therefore, the club will play its home games at Cheltenham Town's Whaddon Road ground. The work involves the construction of four new stands as well as the slight relocation of the pitch to the east.

The 2006/07 season proved to a highly successful one for the city of Bristol, with both teams achieving promotion, although for Rovers it was via the longer route of the Play-Offs from League Two. Under Paul Trollope, a late burst of form saw the team snatch one of the Play-Off places, although it did require a final day victory over already promoted Hartlepool at the Victoria Ground to take Rovers up to sixth place and a semi-final against serial Play-Off participants Lincoln City. Victory over the two legs took Rovers to Wembley to face Shrewsbury Town; backed by some 40,000 Bristolians, the Pirates initially fell behind but by half time were 2-1 up and, despite all the pressure from the Shrews in the second half, Rovers ended up winning 3-1. As a team going up through the Play-Offs — particularly one that finished 13 points adrift of the automatic promotion places — Rovers will be considered as one of the weaker promoted teams and will, therefore, potentially face a battle for survival. However, provided that Trollope can strengthen his squad, the Pirates should have the potential to ensure the team's League One status although it could go either way.

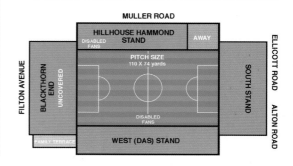

C Rugby Club offices
E Entrance(s) for visiting supporters
R Refrshments for visiting supporters
T Toilets for visiting supporters

1 Filton Avenue
2 Gloucester Road
3 To Muller Road
4 To Bristol city centre (2.5 miles) and BR Temple Meads station (3 miles)
5 Downer Road
6 Car Park
7 To M32 J2 (1.5 miles)
8 Strathmore Road
9 To Filton (1.5 miles)
10 Hill House Hammond Stand
11 West (Das) Stand
12 Blackthorn End
13 South Stand

↘ North direction (approx)

◄ 700378
▼ 700373

Burnley

Turf Moor
Harry Potts Way, Burnley, Lancs, BB10 4BX

Tel No: 0870 443 1882

Advance Tickets Tel No: 0870 443 1914

Fax: 01282 700014

Web Site:
www.burnleyfootballclub.premium.co.uk

E-Mail: info@burnleyfc.com

League: League Championship

Last Season: 15th (P46; W 15; D 12; L 19; GF 52; GA 49)

Training Ground: Gawthorpe Hall, Off Padiham Road, Padiham, Burnley BB12 8UA

Nickname: The Clarets

Brief History: Founded 1882, Burnley Rovers (Rugby Club) combined with another Rugby Club, changed to soccer and name to Burnley. Moved from Calder Vale to Turf Moor in 1882. Founder-members Football League (1888). Record attendance 54,775

(Total) Current Capacity: 22,546 (all seated)

Visiting Supporters' Allocation: 4,125 (all seated in David Fishwick [Cricket Field] Stand)

Club Colours: Claret and blue shirts, white shorts

Nearest Railway Station: Burnley Central

Parking (Car): Church Street and Fulledge Rec. (car parks)

Parking (Coach/Bus): As directed by Police

Police Force and Tel No: Lancashire (01282 425001)

Disabled Visitors' Facilities:
Wheelchairs: Places available in North, East and Cricket Field stands
Blind: Headsets provided with commentary

Anticipated Development(s): The club has proposals for the redevelopment of the Cricket Field (David Fishwick) Stand but this depends on the relocation of the cricket club. The new structure would provide seating for some 7,000. In the event of this option not proving practical attention will turn to the expansion of the Bob Lord Stand.

A modest advance on the position achieved in 2005/06 saw Steve Cotterill's team move up to 15th in the Championship although for the Clarets there was relatively little to celebrate during a fairly disappointing season, particularly as the early part of the season had seemed to promise some success on the field. Although never directly threatened with relegation, the club's gradual drift down the table and position just above the drop zone meant that a couple of bad results could have resulted in the team being sucked into the battle. Away from the league, Burnley suffered the embarrassment of a 1-0 home defeat by League Two outfit Hartlepool in the first round of the Carling Cup. For 2007/08 Burnley should again secure their League Championship position but with a number of well-funded teams at the top — including the three relegated from the Premier League with their parachute payments — it's likely that Burnley will struggle to make a serious challenge for the Play-Offs.

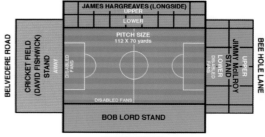

C Club Offices
S Club Shop
E Entrance(s) for visiting
  supporters

1 Brunshaw Road
2 Belvedere Road
3 Burnley Central BR
  Station (½ mile)
4 Cricket Ground
5 Cricket Field Stand
6 East (Jimmy McIlroy)
  Stand
7 Bob Lord Stand
8 North (James Hargreaves)
  Stand

➘ North direction (approx)

◄ 700153
▼ 700160

Bury

Gigg Lane
Lancashire, BL9 9HR

Tel No: 0161 764 4881

Advance Tickets Tel No: 0161 705 2144

Fax: 0161 764 5521

Web Site: www.buryfc.co.uk

E-Mail: info@buryfc.co.uk

League: League Two

Last Season: 21st
(P 46; W 13; D 11; L 22; GF 46; GA 61)

Training Ground: Lower Gigg, Gigg Lane, Bury BL9 9HR

Brief History: Founded 1885, no former names or former grounds. Record attendance 35,000

(Total) Current Capacity: 11,669 (all seated)

Visiting Supporters' Allocation: 2,500 (all seated) in Cemetery End Stand

Club Colours: White shirts, royal blue shorts

Nearest Railway Station: Bury Interchange

Parking (Car): Street parking

Parking (Coach/Bus): As directed by Police

Police Force and Tel No: Greater Manchester (0161 872 5050)

Other clubcs sharing ground: FC United of Manchester

Disabled Visitors' Facilities:
Wheelchairs: South Stand (home) and West Stand (away)
Blind: Commentary available

Anticipated Development(s): The completion of the rebuilt Cemetery End means that current plans for the redevelopment of Gigg Lane have been completed.

One of a number of teams struggling to avoid the drop from League Two, the Shakers under Chris Casper again battled hard and had secured their status before the final weekend of the season — albeit only just. A poor start to the campaign, with the team losing seven of its first nine league matches was offset in part by a triumph over League Championship side Sunderland in the first round of the Carling Cup (although, to be fair, Sunderland itself was struggling at that stage of the season for form as well), was matched by an equally depressing run towards the end of the season with only two draws and one win in the final six matches, which saw the team drop two places from 19th to 21st. Fortunately, enough points had been gathered by that stage to avoid any last day dramas, but for 2007/08 Bury is likely again to be a team more concerned about relegation than promotion.

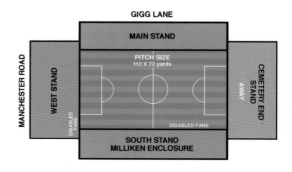

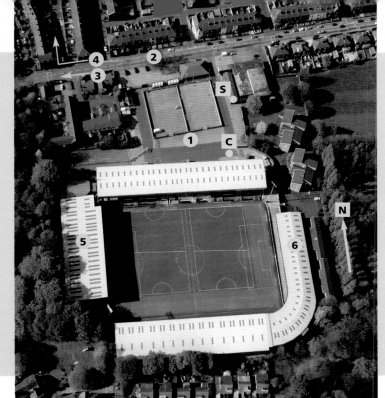

C Club Offices
S Club Shop

1 Car Park
2 Gigg Lane
3 To A56 Manchester Road
4 To Town Centre & Bury
  Interchange (Metrolink)
  (¾ mile)
5 West (Manchester Road)
  Stand
6 Cemetery End (away)

↘ North direction (approx)

◄ 700091
▼ 700097

Cardiff City

Ninian Park
Sloper Road, Cardiff, CF11 8SX

Tel No: 029 2022 1001

Advance Tickets Tel No: 0845 345 1400

Fax: 029 2034 1148

Web Site: www.cardiffcityfc.premiumtv.co.uk

E-mail: club@cardiffcityfc.co.uk

League: League Championship

Last Season: 13th
(P46; W 17; D 13; L 16; GF 57; GA 53)

Training Ground: University of Glamorgan, Tyn-Y-Wern Playing Fields, Treforest Industrial Estate, Upper Boat, Pontypridd, CF37 5UP

Nickname: The Bluebirds

Brief History: Founded 1899. Former Grounds: Riverside Cricket Club, Roath, Sophia Gardens, Cardiff Arms Park and The Harlequins Rugby Ground, moved to Ninian Park in 1910. Ground record attendance 61,566 (Wales v. England, 1961)

(Total) Current Capacity: 20,000 (12,647 seated)

Visiting Supporters' Allocation: 2,000 maximum in John Smiths Grange End Terrace (limited seating)

Club Colours: Blue shirts, blue shorts

Nearest Railway Station: Ninian Park (adjacent) (Cardiff Central 1 mile)

Parking (Car): Opposite Ground, no street parking around ground

Parking (Coach/Bus): Leckwith Stadium car park

Police Force and Tel No: South Wales (029 2022 2111)

Disabled Visitors' Facilities:
Wheelchairs: Corner Canton Stand/Popular Bank (covered)
Blind: No special facility

Anticipated Development(s): After some delays work was due to have commenced on the new 30,000-seat ground in May with an anticipated completion date of February 2009 following the go-ahead from the council in November 2006. The project, estimated to cost £38million, is being built on the site of the Leckwith athletics stadium and the development will also include a new athletics track as well as retail units.

Ultimately a disappointing season for Dave Jones and his Cardiff City team that had promised so much early on as the team seemed to be pushing either for automatic promotion or for a Play-Off place at the very least. In the event, a position of mid-table mediocrity, finishing below the 11th place achieved in 2005/06, is one that gives cause for concern for the new season, particularly if the form of the latter part of the season is replicated in 2007/08. Cardiff City, with its plans for a new stadium, is an ambitious club and failure to make a significant start to the season could put Jones's position at risk. Looking at the teams in the League Championship, however, it's hard to avoid concluding that whilst City should have the potential to make a decent attempt at the Play-Offs again, the best that fans can look forward to is perhaps a good top-half finish.

C Club Offices
S Club Shop
E Entrance(s) for visiting supporters
R Refreshment bars for visiting supporters
T Toilets for visiting supporters

1 Sloper Road
2 B4267 Leckwith Road
3 Car Park
4 To A4232 & M4 Junction 33 (8 miles)
5 Ninian Park Road
6 To City Centre & Cardiff Central BR Station (1 mile)
7 To A48 Western Avenue, A49M, and M4 Junction 32 and 29
8 Ninian Park BR station

↘ North direction (approx)

◄ 699068
▼ 699079

Carlisle United

Brunton Park
Warwick Road, Carlisle, CA1 1LL

Telephone: 01228 526237

Advance Tickets Tel No: 01228 526327

Fax: 01228 554141

Web Site: www.carlisleunited.premiumtv.co.uk

E-mail: enquiries@carlisleunited.co.uk

League: League One

Last Season: 8th
(P 46; W 19; D 11; L 16; GF 54; GA 55)

Training Ground: Adjacent to main ground

Nickname: The Cumbrians or the Blues

Brief History: Founded 1904 as Carlisle United (previously named Shaddongate United). Former Grounds: Millholme Bank and Devonshire Park, moved to Brunton Park in 1909. Record attendance 27,500

(Total) Current Capacity: 16,981 (6,433 seated)

Visiting Supporters' Allocation: 1,700 (Petterill End Terrace — open — or north end of Main Stand)

Club Colours: Blue shirts, white shorts

Nearest Railway Station: Carlisle

Parking (Car): Rear of ground

Parking (Coach/Bus): St Aiden's Road car park

Police Force and Tel No: Cumbria (01228 528191)

Disabled Visitors' Facilities:

Wheelchairs: East Stand and Paddock (prior arrangement)

Blind: No special facilities

Anticipated Development(s):

Having been promoted at the end of 2005/06 and having lost manager Paul Simpson, who had guided the team to two successive promotions, a season of consolidation under new manager Neil McDonald might have been expected at Brunton Park. In the event, however, the Blues had a remarkably successful campaign ultimately, finishing in eight place, just outside the Play-Off zone. For the new season, there is every indication that United will again feature in the battle for the Play-Off places.

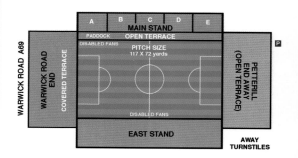

C Club Offices
E Entrance(s) for visiting supporters
R Refreshment bars for visiting supporters
T Toilets for visiting supporters

1 A69 Warwick Road
2 To M6 Junction 43
3 Carlisle Citadel BR station (1 mile)
4 Greystone Road
5 Car Park
6 Petterill End (away)
7 Cumberland Bulding Society (East) Stand

↘ North direction (approx)

◄ 699882
▼ 699091

The Valley
Floyd Road, Charlton, London, SE7 8BL

Tel No: 020 8333 4000

Advance Tickets Tel No: 0871 226 1905

Fax: 020 8333 4001

Web Site: www.cafc.co.uk

E-Mail: info@cafc.co.uk

League: League Championship

Last Season: 19th (relegated)
(P 38; W 8; D 10; L 20; GF 34; GA 60)

Training Ground: Sparrows Lane, New Eltham, London SE9 2JR

Nickname: The Addicks

Brief History: Founded 1905. Former grounds: Siemens Meadows, Woolwich Common, Pound Park, Angerstein Athletic Ground, The Mount Catford, Selhurst Park (Crystal Palace FC), Boleyn Ground (West Ham United FC), The Valley (1912-23, 1924-85, 1992-date). Founder Members 3rd Division South. Record attendance 75,031

(Total) Current Capacity: 27,116 (all seated)

Visiting Supporters' Allocation: 3,000 (maximum; all seated in South Stand)

Club Colours: Red shirts, white shorts

Nearest Railway Station: Charlton

Parking (Car): Street parking

Parking (Coach/Bus): As directed by Police

Police Force and Tel No: Metropolitan (020 8853 8212)

Disabled Visitors' Facilities:
Wheelchairs: East/West/South stands
Blind: Commentary, 12 spaces

Anticipated Development(s): The club presented plans to Greenwich Council in mid-December 2006 for the redevelopment of the East Stand, taking the ground's capacity to 31,000. At the same time the club lodged outline plans for the redevelopment of the rest of the stadium with the intention of taking capacity to 40,600.

The first Premiership management casualty of the season was Iain Dowie, who lasted 12 league games at The Valley before he was dismissed in mid-November following a 3-2 reverse at Wigan, a result that meant that the Addicks had only won two league games under Dowie and were rooted to the bottom of the table. Les Reed took over as caretaker initially before being confirmed in his position on a permanent basis. However, despite signing a long-term contract, Reed's departure was announced on Christmas Eve following an embarrassing home defeat by Wycombe in the Carling Cup quarter finals and a run in the league of seven games with only one victory. Ex-Hammers' boss Alan Pardew was quickly appointed, thus becoming the Addicks' third manager of the season. However, Pardew was unable to reverse the drift towards relegation and the drop was confirmed before the final weekend. As with other teams relegated from the Premier League, the club will have the benefit of the parachute payments for two years and, provided that the nucleus of the team can be kept together, ought to be able to be serious candidates for promotion at the end of 2007/08. Of the three teams relegated at the end of 2005/06, two were promoted automatically and the third made the Play-Offs. However, it looks as though a number of Charlton's squad will be departing and this can only weaken the team. However, despite this, the Addicks should certainly feature in the Championship promotion race.

E   Entrance(s) for visiting supporters
R   Refreshment bars for visiting supporters
T   Toilets for visiting supporters

1   Harvey Gardens
2   A206 Woolwich Road
3   Valley Grove
4   Floyd Road
5   Charlton BR Station
6   East Stand
7   North Stand
8   West stand
9   South stand (away)
10 Charlton Church Lane
11 Charlton Lane

↘ North direction (approx)

◄ 699307
▼ 699295

Chelsea

Stamford Bridge
Fulham Road, London, SW6 1HS

Tel No: 0870 300 2322

Advance Tickets Tel No: 0870 300 2322

Fax: 020 7381 4831

E-Mail: No contact available for general inquiries via e-mail

Web Site: www.chelseafc.com

League: F.A. Premier

Last Season: 2nd
(P 38; W 24; D 11; L 3; GF 64; GA 24)

Training Ground: 62 Stoke Road, Cobham, Surrey KT11 3PT

Nickname: The Blues

Brief History: Founded 1905. Admitted to Football League (2nd Division) on formation. Stamford Bridge venue for F.A. Cup Finals 1919-22. Record attendance 82,905

(Total) Current Capacity: 42,449 (all seated)

Visiting Supporters' Allocation: Approx. 1,600 (East Stand Lower; can be increased to 3,200 if required or 5,200 if part of the Matthew Harding Stand [lower tier] is allocated)

Club Colours: Blue shirts, blue shorts

Nearest Railway Station: Fulham Broadway or West Brompton

Parking (Car): Street parking and underground car park at ground

Parking (Coach/Bus): As directed by Police

Police Force and Tel No: Metropolitan (020 7385 1212)

Disabled Visitors' Facilities:
Wheelchairs: East Stand
Blind: No special facility

Anticipated Development(s): Faced by the competing clubs building ever larger grounds, Chelsea is conscious that the existing 42,000-seat capacity at Stamford Bridge is too small but difficult to increase. As a result the club is examining the possibility of relocation, with a number of sites (including the erstwhile Lillie Bridge cricket ground now used as the Seagrave Road car park as one option). There is, however, no definite plan as yet nor any timetable for the work if it were to proceed.

Despite the high profile arrival of Michael Ballack and Andrei Shevchenko prior to the start of the season, all was not right with the Chelsea ship in 2006/07 with rumours abounding about a falling out between Roman Abramovitch and Jose Mourinho and doubts as to whether the Portuguese manager would still be in his job come the start of the new season. On the field the team came away with two trophies — the Carling Cup and the FA Cup — which would be counted as success for most teams but with expectations high at Stamford Bridge, the failure to land the Premier League title for a third time and defeat in the Champions League semi-finals (against old rivals Liverpool), means that the 2006/07 season was not the greatest. Undoubtedly the squad will be further strengthened during the course of the close season and the team will again certainly be one of the favourites to land the title. The big project, though, has to be the Champions League; should the team look like failing to make it again then Mourinho's position looks increasingly untenable.

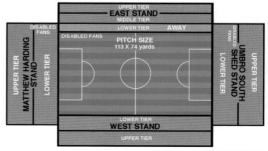

FULHAM ROAD

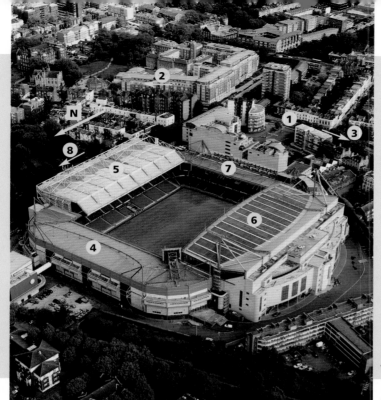

1 A308 Fulham Road
2 Central London
3 To Fulham Broadway
   Tube Station
4 Mathew Harding Stand
5 East Stand
6 West Stand
7 South (Shed) Stand
8 West Brompton Station

↘ North direction (approx)

◄ 700208
▼ 700211

Cheltenham Town

Whaddon Road
Cheltenham, Gloucestershire GL52 5NA

Tel No: 01242 573558

Advance Tickets Tel No: 01242 573558

Fax: 01242 224675

Web Site:
www.cheltenhamtownfc.premiumtv.co.uk

E-Mail: info@ctfc.com

League: League One

Last Season: 17th (P 46; W 15; D 9; L 22; GF 49;
GA 61)

Training Ground: Cheltenham Town FC Training
Complex, Quat Goose Lane, Swindon Village,
Cheltenham GL51 9RX

Nickname: The Robins

Brief History: Cheltenham Town was founded
in 1892. It moved to Whaddon Road in 1932
having previously played at Carter's Field.
After two seasons in the Conference it
achieved Nationwide League status at the
end of the 1998/99 season. Record
attendance 8,326

(Total) Current Capacity: 7,066 (3,912 seated)

Visiting Supporters' Allocation: 2,600
(maximum) in Carlsberg (Whaddon Road)
Stand – and in Wymans Road (In2Print) Stand

Club Colours: Red and white striped shirts,
white shorts

Nearest Railway Station: Cheltenham
(1.5 miles)

Parking (Car): Limited parking at ground;
otherwise on-street

Parking (Coach/Bus): As directed by Police

Police Force and Tel No: Gloucestershire
(01242 521321)

Disabled Visitors' Facilities:
Wheelchairs: Six spaces in front of Main
Stand
Blind: No special facility

Anticipated Development(s): The Carlsberg
stand — which replaced the open Whaddon
Road Terrace — was opened in December
2005. This structure provides seats for 1,000
fans. The next phase in the development of
Whaddon Road will involve the rebuilding of
the Main Stand, but there is at present no
timescale for this work.

Promoted at the end of the 2005/06 season, the new
campaign was always going to be one of
consolidation for John Ward's Cheltenham Town and
saw the Robins achieve a creditable 17th position
although for much of the season it looked as though
relegation was a serious possibility. In the event,
however, the team finished some seven points above
relegated Chesterfield and can look forward to a
further season in League One. Whilst the other Robins
in the division — Bristol City — have been promoted to
the Championship, Cheltenham can look forward to
renewing local rivalry with Bristol Rovers; ironically,
the Pirates are due to become Cheltenham's tenants at
Whaddon Road for the second half of the season
whilst Rovers' own ground is redeveloped. Provided
that the team gets off to a good start, Town should
have the potential to make some progress up the
League One table, although a top-half finish is
perhaps the best that the team can look forward to.

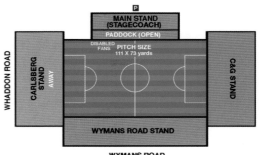

C Club Offices
E Entrance(s) for visiting supporters

1 B4632 Prestbury Road
2 Cromwell Road
3 Whaddon Road
4 Wymans Road
5 To B4075 Priors Road
6 To B4075 Prior Road
7 To Cheltenham town centre and railway station (1.5 and 2 miles respectively)
8 Main Stand
9 Wymans Road Stand
10 Prestbury Road End
11 Carlsberg Stand (away)

↘ North direction (approx)

◀ 699755
▾ 699762

Chester City

Saunders Honda Stadium
Bumpers Lane, Chester, CH1 4LT

Tel No: 01244 371376

Advance Tickets Tel No: 01244 371376

Fax: 01244 390265

Web-site: www.chestercityfc.net

E-mail: Contact via web-site

League: League Two

Last Season: 18th (P 46; W 13; D 14; L 19; GF 40; GA 48)

Training Ground: Chester Catholic High School

Nickname: The Blues

Brief History: Founded 1884 from amalgamation of Chester Wanderers and Chester Rovers. Former Grounds: Faulkner Street, Lightfoot Street, Whipcord Lane, Sealand Road Moss Lane (Macclesfield Town FC), moved to Deva Stadium 1992. Record attendance (Sealand Road) 20,500; (Deva Stadium) 5,987

(Total) Current Capacity: 6,012 (3,284) seated

Visiting Supporters' Allocation: 1,896 maximum (seated 600 maximum) in South Terrace and West Stand

Club Colours: Blue/White striped shirts, Blue shorts

Nearest Railway Station: Chester (three miles)

Parking (Car): Car park at ground

Parking(Coach/Bus): Car park at ground

Police Force and Tel No: Cheshire (01244 350222)

Disabled Visitors' Facilities:

Wheelchairs: West and East Stand

Blind: Facility available

Anticipated Development(s):

At the end of April, manager Mark Wright and assistant Graham Barrow were sacked following a dismal run of only three wins in 20 games, a sequence that left the team in 18th position. Youth team manager Simon Davies was appointed caretaker boss to oversee the team for the last match of the season. For Wright, who had been boss at the Deva Stadium since February 2006, it was the end of his second spell as manager of the team. Under the new management, the club's League Two status was secured although the team finished — in 18th position — exactly where Davies had inherited it. After the season ended it was announced that experienced manager Bobby Williamson had been appointed manager. One issue that Williamson will need to address if the team isn't again going to struggle is up front, with the team only scoring 40 league goals all season. If the team can improve on this, then a mid-table position in 2007/08 should be achievable; if not, then a battle against a return to the Conference looks likely.

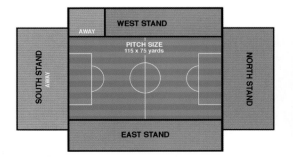

C Club Offices
S Club Shop
E Entrance(s) for visiting
  supporters
R Refreshment bars for
  visiting supporters
T Toilets for visiting
  supporters

1 Bumpers Lane
2 To City centre and Chester
  railway station (1.5 miles)
3 Car park
4 South Terrace
5 West Stand

↘ North direction (approx)

◀ 700510
▼ 700517

Chesterfield

Recreation Ground
Saltergate, Chesterfield, S40 4SX

Tel No: 01246 209765

Advance Tickets Tel No: 01246 209765

Fax: 01246 556799

Web Site: www.chesterfield-fc.premiumtv.co.uk

E-Mail: suegreen@therecreationground.co.uk

League: League Two

Last Season: 21st (relegated) (P 46; W 12; D 11; L 23; GF 45; GA 53)

Training Ground: No special facility

Nickname: The Spireites

Brief History: Found 1886. Former Ground: Spital Vale. Formerly named Chesterfield Town. Record attendance 30,968

(Total) Current Capacity: 8,504 (2,674 seated)

Visiting Supporters' Allocation: 1,850 maximum (maximum 450 seated)

Club Colours: Blue and white shirts, white shorts

Nearest Railway Station: Chesterfield

Parking (Car): Saltergate car park, street parking

Parking (Coach/Bus): As directed by Police

Police Force and Tel No: Derbyshire (01246 220100)

Disabled Visitors' Facilities:
Wheelchairs: Saltergate Stand
Blind: No special facility

Anticipated Development(s): The club is progressing with plans for the construction of a new 10,600-seat ground on the site of the closed Dema glassworks on the A61. However, physical work on the site has been delayed as a result of land ownership for part of the site. Despite this, the club remains hopeful that the new ground will be completed in time for the start of the 2008/09 season.

The managerial roundabout rolled into Saltergate in mid-March when, after a run of four straight defeats and one victory in 10 matches, Roy McFarland left the Spireites after almost four years in charge. Lee Richardson was immediately appointed as caretaker manager until the end of the season although he was confirmed as full-time boss before the end of the campaign. He took over with the club standing in 20th place, one point above the drop zone. Unfortunately for Richardson, he wasn't able to prevent Chesterfield slipping into the drop zone although it was not until the penultimate series of matches that relegation was confirmed. Away from the league, the Spirites had some success in the Carling Cup — defeating Championship side Wolves at home on penalties in round one and Premier League Manchester City 2-1 at Saltergate in round two — before discovering that the giantkilling act could work both ways when non-league Basingstoke won 1-0 at Saltergate in the first round of the FA Cup. In terms of the 2007/08 season, Richardson will take heart from the fact that all three of the teams promoted automatically from League Two at the end of 2006/07 had been relegated the previous year and would expect his team to emulate this. Chesterfield should certainly feature in the battle for either automatic promotion or the Play-Offs at worst.

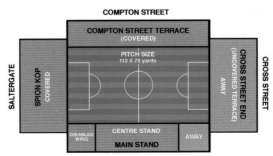

C Club Offices
S Club Shop
E Entrance(s) for visiting supporters
R Refreshment bars for visiting supporters
T Toilets for visiting supporters

1 Saltergate
2 Cross Street
3 St Margaret's Drive
4 West Bars
5 To A617 & M1 Junction 29
6 To station and town centre
7 Compton Street Terrace
8 Cross Street End (away)

↘ North direction (approx)

◀ 699864
▼ 699877

Colchester United

Layer Road Ground
Colchester, CO2 7JJ

Tel No: 0871 2262161

Advance Tickets Tel No: 081 226 2161

Fax: 01206 715327

Web Site: www.cu-fc.premiumtv.co.uk

E-Mail: caroline@colchesterunited.net

League: League Championship

Last Season: 10th
(P 46; W 20; D 9; L 17; GF 70; GA 56)

Training Ground: No special facility

Nickname: The U's

Brief History: Founded 1937, joined Football League 1950, relegated 1990, promoted 1992. Record attendance 19,072

(Total) Current Capacity: 6,200 (1,877 seated)

Visiting Supporters' Allocation: 650 in Layer Road End (standing) plus 200 seats (East Coast Cable Stand)

Club Colours: Royal blue and white shirts, blue shorts

Nearest Railway Station: Colchester Town

Parking (Car): Street parking

Parking (Coach/Bus): Boadicea Way

Police Force and Tel No: Essex (01206 762212)

Disabled Visitors' Facilities:
Wheelchairs: Space for 12 in front of terrace (next to Main Stand)
Blind: Space for 3 blind persons and 3 guides (two regularly occupied by home supporters)

Anticipated Development(s): In mid-November it was announced that the local council had agreed to borrow the finance required to construct the £14 million 10,000-seat community stadium planned for the Cuckoo Farm site. If all had gone according to plan, United were planning to move into the new ground in the early part of 2008; however, delays in the legal documentation in early 2007 means that this date will not be met. Work started on the new stand at the end of July 2007.

A season of considerable success for Colchester United, playing in the second tier of English football for the first time in the club's history, saw the U's seriously threaten for a Play-Off position for much of the campaign — indeed if results had gone the club's way towards the end of the season, the team might easily have sneaked in. Under Geraint Williams, appointed during the summer of 2006, the team performed strongly, particularly at home, and proved most pundits wrong when they suggested that the team might make an immediate return to League One. Such was the teams' initial impact that a number of commentators were speculating about whether Layer Road would be permitted to host Premier League football. One result that will have given immense satisfaction at Layer Road was the 5-1 drubbing of Hull City, a team managed at that stage by ex-United boss Phil Parkinson, who left in controversial circumstances during the summer of 2006. However, the second season at this higher level may prove more difficult and, rather than believing that that the Play-Offs are within striking distance the club's ambitions may be better suited to a further season of consolidation. Moreover, the close season saw the departure of one of the club's main strikers — Chris Iwelumo — and with fellow striker Jamie Cureton following suit, the club may struggle for goals in 2007/08. With Layer Road's limited capacity, the club will be at a financial disadvantage to most of the competition and perhaps a reality check may come as no bad thing.

C Club Offices
S Club Shop
E Entrance(s) for visiting supporters
R Refreshment bars for visiting supporters
T Toilets for visiting supporters

1 B1026 Layer Road
2 Town Centre & Colchester Town BR Station (2 miles)
3 Evening Gazette Main Stand
4 Barside Popular Side
5 East Coast Cable Stand

↘ North direction (approx)

◄ 700744
▼ 700753

The Ricoh Arena
Phoenix Way, Foleshill, Coventry CV6 6GE

Telephone: 0870 421 1987

Advance Tickets Tel No: 0870 421 1987

Fax: 0870 421 5073

Web Site: www.ccfc.premiumtv.co.uk

E-mail: info@ccfc.co.uk

League: League Championship

Last Season: 17th
(P46; W 16; D 8; L 22; GF 47; GA 62)

Training Ground: Sky Blue Lodge, Leamington Road, Ryton-on-Dunsmore, Coventry CV8 3EL

Nickname: The Sky Blues

Brief History: Founded 1883 as Singers FC, changed name to Coventry City in 1898. Former grounds: Dowell's Field, Stoke Road Ground and Highfield Road (1899-2005) moved to new ground for start of the 2005/06 season. Record attendance (at Highfield Road): 51,455; (at Ricoh Stadium) 28,120

(Total) Current Capacity: 32,500

Visiting Supporters' Allocation: 3,000 in corner of Jewson South and Telnet West Stands

Club Colours: sky blue shirts, sky blue shorts

Nearest Railway Station: Coventry (three miles)

Parking (Car): As directed

Parking (Coach/Bus): As directed

Police Force and Tel No: West Midlands (02476 539010)

Disabled Visitors' Facilities:

Wheelchairs: 102 spaces (including 27 away) at pitchside or raised platform

Blind: no special facility at present but under negotiation

Anticipated Development(s): With the completion of the Ricoh Stadium there are no further plans for development at the present time. There is still no news about the construction of a possible station on the Coventry-Nuneaton railway line.

With City struggling in the Championship and following an embarrassing 2-0 home defeat to League One outfit Bristol City in the FA Cup Third Round replay, Micky Adams was sacked as manager in mid-January. He was replaced on a caretaker basis by Adrian Heath before the club moved to appoint Iain Dowie, following his brief spell in charge at Charlton, in mid-February. Under Dowie, the club retained its League Championship status, ultimately finishing in 17th place, but it's hard to escape the conclusion that, as the League Championship gets ever more competitive at the top, erstwhile Premier League teams such as Coventry, now operating beyond the period of parachute payments, will struggle to make an impact. Away from the league, the Sky Blues suffered an embarrassing 3-1 defeat away at Hereford United in the first round of the Carling Cup. In 2007/08 a top half finish should undoubtedly be within the team's reach but the Play-Offs and automatic promotion appear well beyond the team's capabilities.

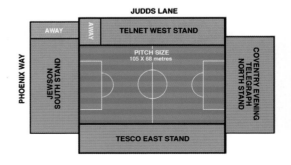

1 Judds Lane
2 Rowley's Green Lane
3 A444 Phoenix Way
4 To Coventry city centre and BR railway station (three miles)
5 Coventry-Nuneaton railway line
6 To M6 Junction 3 (one mile) and Nuneaton
7 Marconi West Stand
8 Coventry Evening Telegraph North Stand
9 NTL East Stand
10 Jewson South Stand
11 Exhibition hall and planned casino

↘ North direction (approx)

◂ 699766
▾ 699769

Crewe Alexandra

The Alexandra Stadium
Gresty Road, Crewe, Cheshire, CW2 6EB

Tel No: 01270 213014

Advance Tickets Tel No: 01270 252610

Fax: 01270 216320

Website: www.crewealex.premiumtv.co.uk

E-Mail: info@crewealex.net

League: League One

Last Season: 13th
(P 46; W 17; D 9; L 20; GF 66; GA 72)

Training Ground: Details omitted at club's request

Nickname: The Railwaymen

Brief History: Founded 1877. Former Grounds: Alexandra Recreation Ground (Nantwich Road), Earle Street Cricket Ground, Edleston Road, Old Sheds Fields, Gresty Road (Adjacent to current Ground), moved to current Ground in 1906. Founder members of 2nd Division (1892) until 1896. Founder members of 3rd Division North (1921). Record attendance 20,000

(Total) Current Capacity: 10,100 all seated

Visiting Supporters' Allocation: 1,694 (Blue Bell BMW Stand)

Club Colours: Red shirts, white shorts

Nearest Railway Station: Crewe

Parking (car): There is a car park adjacent to the ground. It should be noted that there is a residents' only scheme in operation in the streets surrounding the ground.

Parking (Coach/Bus): As directed by Police

Police Force and Tel No: Cheshire (01270 500222)

Disabled Visitors' Facilities:
Wheelchairs: Available on all four sides
Blind: Commentary available

Anticipated Development(s): The club has long term plans for the construction of a new two-tier stand to replace the Blue Bell (BMW) Stand, although there is no confirmed timescale for the work.

Unlike the previous occasion when Crewe dropped back into League One and made an immediate return to the Championship, Dario Gradi's team found the competition at this level in 2006/07 much stronger and the team never made a serious bid for either automatic promotion of the Play-Offs. Gradi, however, as befits the manager with the longest one-club career in the Football League, is an astute operator and undoubtedly will use the close season to strengthen his squad carefully, with the result that the Railwaymen should probably be one of those vying for a Play-Off place come the end of the season. Away from the league, Crewe had one excellent result in the Carling Cup, defeating Wigan Athletic 2-0 at Gresty Road in the second round, although a 4-0 reverse at League One strugglers Bradford City in the FA Cup was less positive.

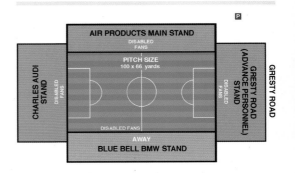

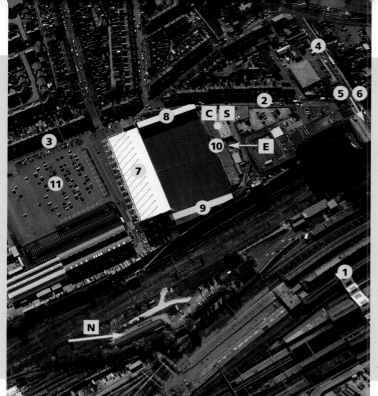

C Club Offices
S Club Shop
E Entrance(s) for visiting
  supporters

1 Crewe BR Station
2 Gresty Road
3 Gresty Road
4 A534 Nantwich Road
5 To A5020 to
  M6 Junction 16
6 To M6 Junction 17 [follow
  directions at roundabout
  to M6 J16/J17]
7 Main (Air Products) Stand
8 Gresty Road (Advance
  Personnel) Stand
9 Charles Audi Stand
10 Ringways Stand
  (Blue Bell BMW)(away)
11 Car Park

↘ North direction (approx)

◂ 699095
▾ 699100

Selhurst Park
London, SE25 6PU

Tel No: 020 8768 6000

Advance Tickets Tel No: 08712 000071

Fax: 020 8771 5311

Web Site: www.cpfc.premiumtv.co.uk

E-Mail: info@cpfc.co.uk

Ticket Office/Fax: 020 8653 4708

League: League Championship

Last Season: 12th
(P 46; W 18; D 11; L 17; GF 59; GA 51)

Training Ground: Copers Cope Road, Beckenham BR3 1RJ

Nickname: The Eagles (historically the Glaziers)

Brief History: Founded 1905. Former Grounds: The Crystal Palace (F.A. Cup Finals venue), London County Athletic Ground (Herne Hill), The Nest (Croydon Common Athletic Ground), moved to Selhurst Park in 1924. Founder members 3rd Division (1920). Record attendance 51,482

(Total) Current Capacity: 26,300 all seated

Visiting Supporters' Allocation: Approx 2,000 in Arthur Wait Stand

Club Colours: Blue and red striped shirts, blue shorts

Nearest Railway Station: Selhurst, Norwood Junction and Thornton Heath

Parking (Car): Street parking and Sainsbury's car park

Parking (Coach/Bus): Thornton Heath

Police Force and Tel No: Metropolitan (020 8653 8568)

Disabled Visitors' Facilities:
Wheelchairs: 56 spaces in Arthur Wait and Holmesdale Stands
Blind: Commentary available

Anticipated Development(s): Although the club had plans to reconstruct the Main Stand — indeed had Planning Permission for the work — local opposition has meant that no work has been undertaken. Serious thought is now being given to relocation. The long-running split between ownership of the ground and ownership of the club was resolved in October when Simon Jordan acquired the freehold of Selhurst Park from Ron Noades for £12 million.

Following the departure of Iain Dowie, in controversial circumstances and for which Simon Jordan took successful legal action, Peter Taylor took over before the start of the season. Under Taylor's management, the Eagles had a relatively disappointing second season back in the Championship following the success of reaching the Play-Offs at the end on 2005/06 and there were mutterings about the manager during the season. The season started brightly enough with three straight league wins, but the team was too inconsistent to maintain a serious challenge and there were periods during the season when the team struggled to gain a victory — a series of eight matches between the end of September and the middle of November being symptomatic — and there was a real risk of the Eagles being sucked into the relegation battle. However, the club eventually amassed enough points to achieve a position of mid-table mediocrity. Away from the league, indications of the club's playing fortunes were highlighted in the 2-1 home defeat by League Two Notts County in the first round of the Carling Cup. For 2007/08, with the Premier League's parachute payments now a thing of the past, Palace may well again struggle to sustain a push for anything other than a further mid-table position. At present, Jordan is sticking with Taylor in the hot-seat; for how long will depend on the start that the Eagles make in the new season.

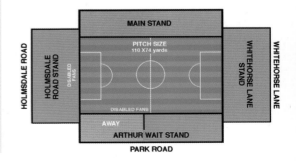

C Club Offices
S Club Shop
E Entrance(s) for visiting
  supporters
T Toilets for visiting
  supporters

1 Whitehorse Lane
2 Park Road
3 Arthur Wait Stand Road
4 Selhurst BR Station
  (½ mile)
5 Norwood Junction BR
  Station (¼ mile)
6 Thornton Heath BR
  Station (½ mile)
7 Car Park (Sainsbury's)

↘ North direction (approx)

◄ 700223
▼ 700220

Dagenham & Redbridge

Glyn Hopkin Stadium
Victoria Road, Dagenham, Essex RM10 7XL

Telephone: 020 8592 1549
Advance Tickets Tel No: 020 8592 1549
Fax: 020 8593 7227
Web Site: www.daggers.co.uk
E-mail: info@daggers.co.uk
League: League Two
Last Season: 1st (promoted)
  (P 46; W 28; D 11; L 7; GF 93; GA 48)
Training Ground: No special facility
Brief History: The club has roots in four earlier
  clubs: Ilford (1881); Leytonstone (1886);
  Walthamstow Avenue (1900); and Dagenham
  (1949). Ilford and Leytonstone merged in 1979
  and, in 1988, became Redbridge Forest
  following the incorporation of Walthamstow
  Athletic. Redbridge Forest moved to Victoria
  Road in 1991 and formed Dagenham &
  Redbridge with Dagenham in 1992. Promoted
  to the Football League at the end of the
  2006/07 season. Record attendance (at the
  Victoria Ground): 7,200; (as Dagenham &
  Redbridge): 5,949
(Total) Current Capacity: 6,078
Visiting Supporters' Allocation: 1,200
  (Pondfield open terrace; all standing)
Club Colours: Red and white shirts, red shorts
Nearest Railway Station: Dagenham East
  (District Line)
Parking (Car): car park at ground or on-street
Parking (Coach/Bus): As directed
Police Force and Tel No: Metropolitan
Disabled Visitors' Facilities:
  Wheelchairs: 10 spaces at Pondfield End of
  Main Stand
  Blind: No specific facility
Anticipated Development(s):

After a number of years when the Daggers were there or thereabouts in terms of promotion to the Football League, at the end of the 2006/07 season the team finally achieved League status as John Still's team eventually came to dominate the Nationwide Conference. Initially, it looked as though relegated Oxford United were going to be the main threat to the Daggers, but the Oxfordshire challenge proved to be short-lived as the team from Essex proved too strong, ultimately finishing 14 points clear of their nearest rivals. In a nice piece of irony, one of the teams relegated from League Two was Boston United — a team that had previously pipped Dagenham & Redbridge to membership of the league in controversial circumstances at the end of the 2002/03 season. At the Conference level, the Daggers proved themselves to be free scoring but the club will find League Two defences perhaps a bit meaner. In recent years, teams from the Conference have either prospered — like Yeovil Town — or struggled — like Accrington Stanley. Although the Daggers did, like Stanley the previous year, dominate the Conference, the progression into the League may stretch the club and perhaps a season of consolidation is the best that fans can look forward to.

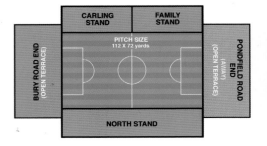

1 A1112 North Rainham Road
2 Dagenham East railway station
3 Oxlow Lane
4 Victoria Road
5 Bury Road
6 Victoria Road
7 North Stand
8 Bury Road Stand
9 Carling Stand
10 Pondfield Road End (away)
11 Family Stand

↘ North direction (approx)

◄ 700788
▼ 700790

Darlington

96.6 TFM Darlington Arena
Neasham Road, Darlington DL2 1DL

Tel No: 01325 387000

Advance Tickets Tel No: 0870 027 2949

Fax: 01325 387050

Web Site: www.darlington-fc.premiumtv.co.uk

E-mail: enquiries@darlington-fc.net

League: League Two

Last Season: 11th
(P46; W 17; D 14; L 15; GF 52; GA 56)

Training Ground: New facility being sought for the 2007/08 season

Nickname: The Quakers

Brief History: Founded 1883. Founder members of 3rd Division (North) 1921. Relegated from 4th Division 1989. Promoted from GM Vauxhall Conference in 1990. Previous Ground: Feethams; moving to Neasham Road in 2003. Record attendance (at Feethams) 21,023; (at Neasham Road) 11,600

(Total) Current Capacity: 27,500

Visiting Supporters' Allocation: 3,000 in East Stand

Club Colours: White and black shirts, black shorts

Nearest Railway Station: Darlington Bank Top

Parking (Car): Spaces available in adjacent car park (£5.00 fee)

Parking (Coach/Bus): As directed

Police Force and Tel No: Durham (01235 467681)

Disabled Visitors Facilities:
Wheelchairs: 165 places
Blind: No special facility

Anticipated Developments: With the construction of the new ground, there are no further plans for development as the existing ground's capacity is more than adequate for League Two.

After almost exactly three years with the club, in his third spell as the Quakers' manager, David Hodgson was initially suspended and then sacked in early October following rumours linking him to the vacant managerial post at Bournemouth. After a brief period with Martin Gray as caretaker-manager, the club appointed ex-Doncaster Rovers' boss Dave Penney to the full-time position at the end of the month. Under Penney the club made steady progress in League Two, ultimately finishing in 11th place six points off the Play-offs. At Doncaster, Penney had considerable success in bringing the South Yorkshire team up from the Conference to League One and with this experience at this level Darlington should do well again in the league in 2007/08 with a Play-off place a possibility. Away from the league, the club had an impressive 2-1 away victory over Stoke City in the first round of the Carling Cup in August.

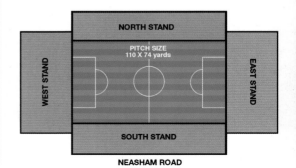

1 A66
2 To Stockton
3 To A66(M) and A1(M)
4 Neasham Road
5 To Darlington town
  centre and railway station
  (one mile)
6 6To Neasham
7 Snipe Lane
8 East Stand (away)

N

↘ North direction (approx)

◀ 700522
▼ 700532

Derby County

Pride Park
Derby, Derbyshire DE24 8XL

Tel No: 0870 444 1884

Advance Tickets Tel No: 0870 444 1884

Fax: 01332 667540

Web Site: www.dcfc.co.uk

E-Mail: derby.county@dcfc.co.uk

League: F.A. Premier

Last Season: 3rd (promoted)
(P46; W 25; D 9; L 14; GF 62; GA 46)

Training Ground: Moor Farm Training Centre,
Morley Road, Oakwood, Derby DE21 4TB

Nickname: The Rams

Brief History: Founded 1884. Former grounds:
The Racecourse Ground, the Baseball Ground
(1894-1997), moved to Pride Park 1997.
Founder members of the Football League
(1888). Record capacity at the Baseball
Ground: 41,826; at Pride Park: 33,597

(Total) Current Capacity: 33,597

Visiting Supporters' Allocation: 4,800
maximum in the South Stand

Club Colours: White shirts and black shorts

Nearest Railway Station: Derby

Parking (Car): 2,300 places at the ground
designated for season ticket holders. Also
two 1,000 car parks on the A6/A52 link road.
No on-street parking

Parking (Coach/Bus): As directed

Police Force and Tel No: Derbyshire (01332
290100)

Disabled Visitors' Facilities:
Wheelchairs: 70 home/30 away spaces
Blind: Commentary available

Anticipated Development(s): Although formal
proposals have yet to be lodged with the
planning authorities, the club is planning a £20
million scheme for a hotel, shops and offices
adjacent to Pride Park.

Following the disastrous season in 2005/06 when the Rams were lucky to retain their League Championship status, 2006/07 proved to be immeasurably more successful. Under former Preston boss, Billy Davies, who'd taken North End into the Play-Offs in two successive seasons, County prospered in the League Championship and fought a close battle with both Birmingham City and Sunderland — both relegated at the end of 2005/06 — for the automatic promotion places right until the penultimate weekend of the season. However, City and Sunderland were to take the automatic places, leaving County to finish third. In the Play-Offs, Derby faced sixth place Southampton and victory over two legs set up a Wembley show down with the third team — West Brom — relegated the previous season. Although the Baggies dominated much of the match, County were to score the only goal, bringing Premier League football back to Pride Park after a number of years. Teams promoted through the Play-Offs have often struggled at the higher level and County will undoubtedly find the Premier League to be a challenge; for the faithful, however, 17th will be regarded as a triumph (and probably as a miracle by anyone else). After the end of the final, Billy Davies threatened that he would leave unless he was granted considerable funds for strengthening; it will be interesting to see how the County story develops over the close season.

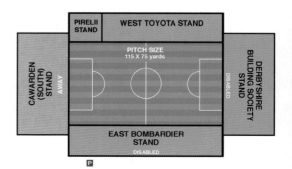

C Club Offices
S Club Shop
E Entrance(s) for visiting supporters

1 To Derby Midland BR station
2 North Stand
3 Toyota West Stand
4 South (Cawarden) Stand (away)
5 Bombardier East Stand
6 Derwent Parade
7 To A52/M1
8 To City Centre and A6

↘ North direction (approx)

◄ 700534
▼ 700544

Doncaster Rovers

Keepmoat Stadium
Stadium Way, Lakeside, Doncaster DN4 5JW

Tel No: 01302 764664

Advance Tickets Tel No: 01302 762576

Fax: 01302 363525

Web Site:
www.doncasterroversfc.premiumtv.co.uk

E-mail: info@doncasterroversfc.co.uk

League: League One

Last Season: 11th
(P46; W 16; D 15; L 15; GF 52; GA 57)

Training Ground: Cantley Park, Aintree Avenue, Doncaster DN4 6HR

Nickname: The Rovers

Brief History: Founded 1879. Former grounds: Town Moor, Belle Vue (not later ground), Deaf school Playing field (later name Intake Ground), Bennetthorpe, Belle Vue (1922-2006). Returned to Football League after a five-year absence in 2003. Record attendance (at Belle Vue) 37,149; (at Keepmoat Stadium) 14,470

(Total) Current Capacity: 15,231

Visiting Supporters' Allocation: 3,350 (North Stand)

Club Colours: Red and white shirts, red shorts

Nearest Railway Station: Doncaster (two miles)

Parking (Car): 1,000 place car park at ground

Parking (Coach/Bus): As directed

Other Clubs Sharing Ground: Doncaster Dragons RLFC and Doncaster Belles Ladies FC

Police Force and Tel No: South Yorkshire (01302 366744)

Disabled Visitors' Facilities:

Wheelchairs: Three sides of ground (16-18 at pitch side)

Blind: Commentary available

Anticipated Development(s): The club moved into the new Keepmoat Stadium during the course of the 2006/07 season. The ground, which cost £21 million to construct, is owned by Doncaster Council. There are no plans for further development at this stage.

At the end of August, having guided the club to its highest league position for some 50 years, Dave Penney announced that he was departing the Belle Vue hot-seat after a five-year spell. During this period he had guided the club from the Conference and League Two into League One, where the club had been on the fringes of the Play-Offs during the 2005/06 season. Following Penney's departure, Mickey Walker took over as caretaker briefly before the club appointed ex-Bournemouth manager Sean O'Driscoll to the position. Under O'Driscoll the club moved into its new Keepmoat Stadium halfway through the season and ultimately finished in 11th place in League One. Apart from progress in the league, Rovers again had some success in the Carling Cup defeating Championship side Derby county on penalties at Belle Vue in the second round. For 2007/08, with the lift that the new ground will give the club, the team should again feature in the battle for the Play-Offs.

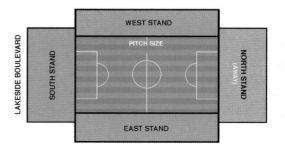

1 Lakeside Boulevard
2 To A6182 White Rose Way
3 To Doncaster town centre and railway station
4 To Junction 3 M18
5 Athletics Stadium
6 Site of 1,000 place car park

N

↘ North direction (approx)

◄ 700553
▼ 700550

Everton

Goodison Park
Goodison Road, Liverpool, L4 4EL

Tel No: 0870 442 1878

Advance Tickets Tel No: 0870 442 1878

Fax: 0151 286 9112

Web Site: www.evertonfc.com

E-Mail: everton@evertonfc.com

League: F.A. Premier

Last Season: 6th
(P 38; W 15; D 13; L 10; GF 52; GA 36)

Training Ground: Bellefield Training Ground, Sandforth Road, West Derby, Liverpool L12 1LW; Tel: 0151 330 2278; Fax: 0151 284 5181

Nickname: The Toffees

Brief History: Founded 1879 as St. Domingo, changed to Everton in 1880. Former grounds: Stanley Park, Priory Road and Anfield (Liverpool F.C. Ground), moved to Goodison Park in 1892. Founder-members Football League (1888). Record attendance 78,299

(Total) Current Capacity: 40,569 all seated

Visiting Supporters' Allocation: 3,000 (part of Bullens Road Stand) maximum

Club Colours: Blue and white shirts, white shorts

Nearest Railway Station: Kirkdale

Parking (Car): Corner of Utting Avenue and Priory Road

Parking (Coach/Bus): Priory Road

Police Force and Tel No: Merseyside (0151 709 6010)

Disabled Visitors' Facilities:
Wheelchairs: Bullens Road Stand
Blind: Commentary available

Anticipated Development(s): With earlier plans for relocation to the King's Dock having been abandoned, the club has developed plans to relocate to a site in Kirkby town centre (adjacent to Knowsley Community College), in the neighbouring borough of Knowsley, where a 55,000-seat ground with other commercial development is planned. There is, however, no confirmed time scale for this work, which is at a very early stage of development and there is also a desire from Liverpool Council to keep the club in the city.

A successful season at Goodison Park saw David Moyes's team in the hunt for a UEFA Cup spot throughout and, in finishing sixth, European football will return to the blue half of Liverpool in 2007/08. Everton, as with a number of Premier League teams, is a club that, at present, is not strong enough to be able to make a sustained challenge for one of the top-four places, but too strong ever to be seriously threatened now with the drop. Each season, a couple of good results can lift the team up the table slightly whereas the following year a couple of poor results can see the team drift towards mid-table. In 2007/08 the team should have the potential again to challenge for a UEFA Cup spot but much will depend on Moyes's ability to retain the core of his existing squad — with rumours at the time of writing that players like Johnson, Cahill and Arteta may be on the move — and on the quality of any replacements.

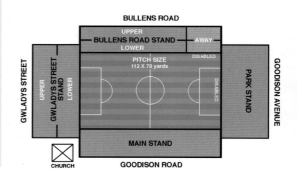

C Club Offices
S Club Shop
E Entrance(s) for visiting
supporters
R Refreshment bars for
visiting supporters
T Toilets for visiting
supporters

1 A580 Walton Road
2 Bullen Road
3 Goodison Road
4 Car Park
5 Liverpool Lime Street BR
Station (2 miles)
6 To M57 Junction 2,
4 and 5
7 Stanley Park
8 Bullens Road Stand
9 Park Stand
10 Main Stand
11 Gwladys Stand

↘ North direction (approx)

◄ 700047
▼ 700053

Fulham

Craven Cottage
Stevenage Road, Fulham, London SW6 6HH

Club Offices: Fulham FC Training Ground, Motspur Park, New Malden, Surrey KT3 6PT

Tel No: 0870 442 1222

Advance Tickets Tel No: 0870 442 1234

Fax: 020 8442 0236

Web-site: www.fulhamfc.com

E-mail: enquiries@fulhamfc.com

League: F.A. Premier

Last Season: 16th
(P38; W 8; D 15; L 15; GF 38;GA 60)

Training Ground: The Academy, Fulham FC, Motspur Park, New Malden, Surrey, KT3 6PT; Tel: 020 8336 7430

Nickname: The Cottagers

Brief History: Founded in 1879 at St. Andrews Fulham, changed name to Fulham in 1898. Former grounds: Star Road, Ranelagh Club, Lillie Road, Eel Brook Common, Purer's Cross, Barn Elms, Half Moon (Wasps Rugby Football Ground), Craven Cottage (from 1894), moved to Loftus Road 2002 and returned to Craven Cottage for start of the 2004/05 season. Record Attendance: Craven Cottage (49,335)

(Total) Current Capacity: 24,600 (all seated)

Visiting Supporters' Allocation: 3,000 in Putney End

Club Colours: White shirts, black shorts

Nearest Railway Station: Putney Bridge (Tube)

Parking (Car): Street parking

Parking(Coach/Bus): Stevenage Road

Police Force and Tel No: Metropolitan (020 7741 6212)

Disabled Visitors' Facilities:
Wheelchairs: Main Stand and Hammersmith End
Blind: No special facility

Anticipated Development(s): Now restored to its traditional home at Craven Cottage, the club is looking either to further develop the ground with a view to obtaining an increased capacity. The most likely route is via the construction of corner infill stands and the rebuilding of the existing stands. There is, however, no confirmed timescale for this work.

After 10 years with the club, as both player and manager, Chris Coleman was sacked as boss after the 3-1 home defeat against Manchester City, a result that saw the Cottagers just four points above an increasingly tight relegation zone following seven games without a win. The manager of Northern Ireland, Lawrie Sanchez, took over as caretaker until the end of the season. Under Sanchez's stewardship, Fulham's Premier League safety was assured before the final match of the season — just as well as Fulham crashed 3-1 in the final match away at Middlesbrough leaving the team two places and one point above relegated Sheffield United. After the end of the season, it was announced that Sanchez had stood down as manager of Northern Ireland and also that he'd take over as Fulham manager on a permanent basis. It was also announced that he would be granted significant funds to strengthen the club's squad. With the three clubs coming up from the League Championship appearing stronger than in recent years, some of the teams that struggled in 2006/07 will have to look to their laurels (or bank managers) if they are to retain Premier League status come the end of the season. Expect another difficult season at Craven Cottage.

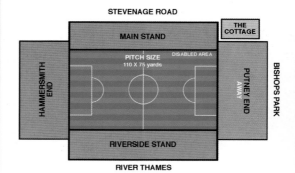

N

E Entrance(s) for visiting
   supporters
R Refreshment bars for
   visiting supporters
T Toilets for visiting
   supporters

1 River Thames
2 Stevenage Road
3 Finlay Street
4 Putney Bridge Tube
   Station (0.5 mile)
5 Putney End (away)
6 Riverside Stand
7 Main Stand
8 Hammersmith End
9 Craven Cottage

↘ North direction (approx)

◄ 700230
▼ 700228

KRBS Priestfield Stadium
Redfern Avenue, Gillingham, Kent, ME7 4DD

Tel No: 01634 300000
Advance Tickets Tel No: 01634 300000
Fax: 01634 850986
Web Site:
   www.gillinghamfootballclub.premiumtv.co.uk
E-mail: info@priestfield.com
League: League One
Last Season: 16th
   (P46; W 17; D 8; L 21; GF 56; GA 77)
Training Ground: Beechings Cross, Grange Road,
   Gillingham ME7 2UD
Nickname: The Gills
Brief History: Founded 1893, as New Brompton,
   changed name to Gillingham in 1913.
   Founder-members Third Division (1920). Lost
   Football League status (1938), re-elected to
   Third Division South (1950). Record
   attendance 23,002
(Total) Current Capacity: 11,582 (all seated)
Visiting Supporters' Allocation: 1,500 (in
   Gillingham (Brian Moore Stand) End)
Club Colours: Blue and black hooped shirts,
   blue shorts
Nearest Railway Station: Gillingham
Parking (Car): Street parking
Parking (Coach/Bus): As directed by Police
Police Force and Tel No: Kent (01634 234488)
Disabled Visitors' Facilities:
   Wheelchairs: Redfern Avenue (Main) Stand
   Blind: No special facility
Anticipated Development(s): The old open
   Town End Terrace was demolished during
   2003 and replaced by a new temporary open
   stand. Planning Permission was granted in
   2003 for the construction of a new 3,500-
   seat stand, to be named after noted fan the
   late Brian Moore, although work has yet to
   commence. Despite the investment at
   Priestfield, however, the club is investigating,
   in conjunction with the local council, the
   possibility of constructing a new stadium at
   Temple Marsh. Towards the end of January,
   chairman Paul Scally announced that he hoped
   to make a statement about relocation within
   six weeks with a view to the club moving to a
   new site within the Medway area for the start
   of the 2010/11 season.

A disappointing season at Priestfield saw the Gills more interested in the battle to avoid the drop rather than the campaign to reclaim a place in the League Championship. Under Ronnie Jepson the team eventually battled to a position of mid-table mediocrity, finishing ultimately in 16th place but the bottom of League One was very tight right until the end of the season and, with the second worst goal difference in the division — only relegated Brentford's was worse — Gillingham had no margin for error. Provided the Jepson is able to strengthen his defence then the Gills should again survive in League One but it could be another season where the team's interests lie towards the wrong end of the division.

E Entrance(s) for visiting
  supporters

1 Redfern Avenue
2 Toronto Road
3 Gordon Road
4 Gillingham BR station
  (¼ mile)
5 Gordon Street Stand
6 New two-tier Main
  (Medway) Stand
7 New Rainham End Stand
8 Gillingham End;
  uncovered seating (away)

↘ North direction (approx)

◄ 700771
▼ 700780

Grimsby Town

Blundell Park
Cleethorpes, DN35 7PY

Tel No: 01472 605050

Advance Tickets Tel No: 01472 605050

Fax: 01472 693665

Web Site: www.grimsby-townfc.premiumtv.co.uk

E-Mail: enquiries@gtfc.co.uk

League: League Two

Last Season: 15th
(P 46; W 17; D 8; L 21; GF 57; GA 73)

Training Ground: Cheapside, Waltham, Grimsby

Nickname: The Mariners

Brief History: Founded in 1878, as Grimsby Pelham, changed name to Grimsby Town in 1879. Former Grounds: Clee Park (two adjacent fields) and Abbey Park, moved to Blundell Park in 1899. Founder-members 2nd Division (1892). Record attendance 31,651

(Total) Current Capacity: 9,546 (all seated)

Visiting Supporters' Allocation: 2,000 in Osmond Stand

Club Colours: Black and white striped shirts, black shorts

Nearest Railway Station: Cleethorpes

Parking (Car): Street parking

Parking (Coach/Bus): Harrington Street

Police Force and Tel No: Humberside (01472 359171)

Disabled Visitors' Facilities:
Wheelchairs: Harrington Street (Main) Stand
Blind: Commentary available

Anticipated Development(s): In late January 2006 it was announced that the club had applied for planning permission to construct a new 20,100-seat ground, to be called the ConocoPhillips Stadium, at Great Coates. Outline planning permission for the work was granted in early 2007. The cost, some £14.4 million, includes a £10 million retail park, with the first phase providing a 12,000-seat facility. Assuming that the outline plans are approved by the local government office, the club has three years to submit detailed plans although it is still aiming for the new ground to be ready for the start of the 2008/09 season.

One of a number of managers appointed during the summer, Graham Rodger's tenure at Grimsby proved to be somewhat curtailed as he was sacked in early November after only five months in the job following a run of six games without a win that left the Mariners in 22nd place in League Two. He was replaced, on a caretaker basis, by Stuart Watkiss, who was later confirmed in the position on a permanent basis. Under Watkiss, the Mariners blew hot and cold, ultimately finishing in 15th place — better than it looked possible at one stage but considerably worse than the 4th place achieved at the end of the 2005/06 season. For 2007/08, Town should have the potential for a top-half finish and the possibility of a decent push for the Play-Offs.

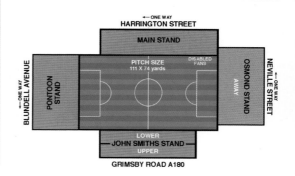

C Club Offices
S Club Shop
E Entrance(s) for visiting
 supporters
R Refreshment bars for
 visiting supporters
T Toilets for visiting
 supporters

1 A180 Grimsby Road
2 Cleethorpes BR Station
 (1½ miles)
3 To Grimsby and M180
 Junction 5
4 Harrington Street
5 Constitutional Avenue
6 Humber Estuary

↘ North direction (approx)

◄ 697766
▼ 697756

Hartlepool United

Victoria Park
Clarence Road, Hartlepool, TS24 8BZ

Tel No: 01429 272584

Advance Tickets Tel No: 01429 272584

Fax: 01429 863007

Web Site:
www.hartlepoolunited.premiumtv.co.uk

E-Mail: enquiries@hartlepoolunited.co.uk

Fax: 01429 863007

League: League One

Last Season: 2nd (promoted)
(P 46; W 26; D 10; L 10; GF 65; GA 40)

Training Ground: Details omitted at club's request

Nickname: The Pool

Brief History: Founded 1908 as Hartlepools United, changed to Hartlepool (1968) and to Hartlepool United in 1977. Founder-members 3rd Division (1921). Record attendance 17,426

(Total) Current Capacity: 7,629 (3,966 seated)

Visiting Supporters' Allocation: 1,000 (located in Rink Stand)

Club Colours: Blue and white striped shirts, blue shorts

Nearest Railway Station: Hartlepool Church Street

Parking (Car): Street parking and rear of clock garage

Parking (Coach/Bus): As directed

Police Force and Tel No: Cleveland (01429 221151

Disabled Visitors' Facilities:
Wheelchairs: Cyril Knowles Stand and Rink End
Blind: Commentary available

Anticipated Development(s): The plans for the redevelopment of the Millhouse Stand are still progressing, although there is now no definite timescale. When this work does commence, the ground's capacity will be reduced to 5,000 temporarily.

One of the four teams relegated from League One at the end of the 2005/06 season, Hartlepool United under Danny Wilson prospered — as did the other three relegated teams — at the lower level and all four were in the hunt for automatic promotion until virtually the end of the season. Fortunately, however, for the Pool, promotion had been secured before the final weekend of the season, although a home defeat against inform Bristol Rovers was to cost the team the chance of the League Two title, which went, instead, to rivals Walsall. The team's good form extended beyond the league as well, with an impressive 1-0 victory away at Championship side Burnley in the first round of the Carling Cup. As a promoted team, the battle will be for Hartlepool to establish themselves at the higher level, but the team has been in League One before and Danny Wilson is an experienced manager at this level. Mind you, few would have prophesied in August 2006 that within 12 months the team would be playing league matches against Leeds United!

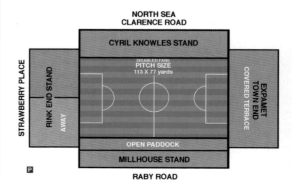

C Club Offices
S Club Shop
E Entrance(s) for visiting
  supporters

1 A179 Clarence Road
2 To Hartlepool Church
  Street BR Station
3 To Marina Way
4 Site of former Greyhound
  Stadium
5 To Middlesbrough A689 &
  A1(M)
6 To A19 North
7 Rink End Stand

↘ North direction (approx)

◄ 700556
▼ 700565

Hereford United

Edgar Street
Hereford, HR4 9JU

Telephone: 01432 276666

Advance Tickets Tel No: 01432 276666

Fax: 01432 341359

Web Site: www.herefordunited.co.uk

E-mail: club@bullsonlilne.co.uk

League: League Two

Last Season: 16th
(P 46; W 14; D 13; L 19; GF 45; GA 53)

Training Ground: No current facility

Nickname: Bulls

Brief History: Founded 1924; first elected to the Football League 1972; relegated to the Conference 1997; promoted through the Play-Offs at the end of 2005/06. Record attendance 18,115

(Total) Current Capacity: 8,843 (1,761 seated)

Visiting Supporters' Allocation: tbc (Floors 2 Go [Edgar Street] Stand and Blackfriards Street End)

Club Colours: White shirts, white shorts

Nearest Railway Station: Hereford

Parking (Car): Merton Meadow and Edgar Street

Parking (Coach/Bus): Cattle Market

Police Force and Tel No: West Mercia (08457 444888)

Disabled Visitors' Facilities:
Wheelchairs: Edgar Street (limited)
Blind: Commentary available

Anticipated Development(s):

Back in the Football League after an absence of almost a decade, Graham Turner's Hereford did better in League Two than the previous season's Conference champions Accrington Stanley and achieved ultimately a position of mid-table security. Away from the league, the club achieved a notable 3-1 victory at Edgar Street in the first round of the Carling Cup against League Championship outfit Coventry City. Never strong enough to mount a challenge for the Play-Offs, having survived the tricky first season back at this level expectations will be high that the team can go further in 2007/08. A top-half finish should be possible.

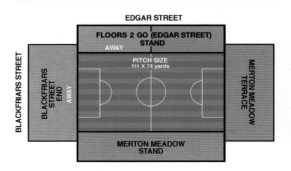

C Club Offices
S Club Shop
E Entrance(s) for visiting
supporters
R Refreshment bars for
visiting supporters
T Toilets for visiting
supporters

1 A49(T) Edgar Street
2 Blackfriars Street
3 Len Weston Stand
4 Merton Meadow Stand
5 Merton Meadow Terrace
6 Blackfriars Street End
7 To Town Centre and
Hereford BR Station

North direction (approx)

◀ 700427
▼ 700436

The Galpharm Stadium
Leeds Road, Huddersfield, HD1 6PX

Tel No: 0870 444 4677

Advance Tickets Tel No: 0870 444 4552

Fax: 01484 484101

Web Site: www.htafc.premiumtv.co.uk

E-Mail: info@htafc.com

League: League One

Last Season: 15th
(P46; W 14; D 17; L 15; GF 60; GA 69)

Training Ground: Storthes Hall, Storthes Hall Lane, Kirkburton, Huddersfield HD8 0WA

Nickname: The Terriers

Brief History: Founded 1908, elected to Football League in 1910. First Club to win the Football League Championship three years in succession. Moved from Leeds Road ground to Kirklees (Alfred McAlpine) Stadium 1994/95 season. Record attendance (Leeds Road) 67,037; Galpharm Stadium: 23,678

(Total) Current Capacity: 24,500 (all seated)

Visiting Supporters' Allocation: 4,037 (all seated)

Club Colours: Blue and white striped shirts, white shorts

Nearest Railway Station: Huddersfield

Parking (Car): Car parks (pre-sold) adjacent to ground

Parking (Coach/Bus): Car parks adjacent to ground

Other Clubs Sharing Ground: Huddersfield Giants RLFC

Police Force and Tel No: West Yorkshire (01484 422122)

Disabled Visitors' Facilities:
Wheelchairs: Three sides of Ground, at low levels and raised area, including toilet access
Blind: Area for partially sighted with Hospital Radio commentary

Anticipated Development(s): With completion of the new North Stand, work on the Galpharm Stadium is over.

Having made the Play-Offs at the end of the 2005/06 season, optimism was high at the Galpharm Stadium that 2006/07 would be the year in which the Terriers achieved promotion. By early March, however, with the team lying in 15th place, 11 points off the Play-Offs, and following a 5-1 drubbing by Nottingham Forest, the club sacked Peter Jackson. Jackson, who'd been with the club for three and a half years in his second spell in charge, was replaced as caretaker boss by Gerry Murphy. The club moved quickly to appoint ex-Barnsley boss Andy Ritchie to the full-time position with the team ultimately finishing in a safe, but disappointing 15th place. For 2007/08, the Terriers have exchanged local derbies against Bradford City for those with Leeds United — just like the old First Division in the 1970s — and it will be interesting to see which of these two comes out on top in the great West Yorkshire championship. Ritchie has experience in getting League One teams promoted — witness his success with Barnsley — and he may well give Huddersfield an edge that they lacked in 2006/07; the team should certainly be capable of a push for the Play-Offs.

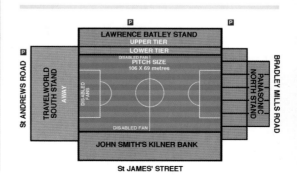

C Club Offices
S Club Shop
E Entrance(s) for visiting
  supporters

1 To Leeds and M62
  Junction 25
2 A62 Leeds Road
3 To Huddersfield BR
  station (1¼ miles)
4 Disabled parking
5 North Stand
6 St Andrews pay car park
7 Coach park
8 South (Pink Link) Stand
  (away)

➘ North direction (approx)

◄ 700079
▼ 700085

Hull City

Kingston Communications Stadium
Walton Street, Hull, East Yorkshire HU3 6HU

Tel No: 0870 837 0003

Advance Tickets Tel No: 0870 837 0004

Fax: 01482 304882

Web Site: www.hullcityafc.premiumtv.co.uk

E-mail: info@hulltigers.com

League: League Championship

Last Season: 21st
(P46; W 13; D 10; L 23; GF 51; GA 67)

Training Ground: Millhouse Woods Lane, Cottingham, Kingston upon Hull HU16 4HB

Nickname: The Tigers

Brief History: Founded 1904. Former grounds: The Boulevard (Hull Rugby League Ground), Dairycoates, Anlaby Road Cricket Circle (Hull Cricket Ground), Anlaby Road, Boothferry Park (from 1946). Moved to Kingston Communications Stadium in late 2002. Record attendance (at Boothferry Park) 55,019; (at Kingston Communications Stadium) 25,280

(Total) Current Capacity: 25,504 (all-seated)

Visiting Supporters' Allocation: 4,000 all-seated in North Stand

Club Colours: Amber shirts, black shorts

Nearest Railway Station: Hull Paragon

Parking (Car): There are 1,800 spaces on the Walton Street Fairground for use on match days

Parking (Coach/Bus): As directed

Other Clubs Sharing Ground: Hull RLFC

Police Force and Tel No: Humberside (01482 220148)

Disabled Visitors' facilities:

Wheelchairs: c300 places

Blind: Contact club for details

Anticipated Development(s): The club moved into the new Kingston Communication Stadium towards the end of 2002. The ground is shared with Hull RLFC. The total cost of the 25,504-seat ground was £44million. The West Stand is provided with two tiers and there are plans for the construction of a second tier on the East and South Stands, taking the capacity to 34,000, if required.

A difficult season for Phil Parkinson's Hull City eventually resulted in the team surviving in the League Championship — just – largely courtesy of the goals scored by the striker Dean Windass on loan from Bradford City (who, ironically, as a result of a lack of strike power up front were ultimately relegated). However, Parkinson, — recruited in controversial circumstances from rivals Colchester United in June 2006 — was not to last long with Hull, being sacked in early December with the club rooted in the relegation zone. He was replaced as caretaker boss by Phil Brown, who was later confirmed in the job on a permanent basis. For much of the season it looked as though the Tigers were going to make a return to League One following two seasons in the Championship and it was only towards the end of the campaign that results started to pick up. After the end of the season it was confirmed that Windass had been transferred from Bradford on a permanent basis, for his second stint at his home city's club and fans of the club will be hoping that the veteran, but prolific, scorer can help raise the club's scoring ability as the club struggled during the 2006/07 season in front of goal. Despite this, however, it's hard to escape the conclusion that once again City will find life in the Championship to be a struggle and relegation could well be a serious threat come May 2008. Hull City was another club to change hands during the year, with Adam Pearson selling out to a new consortium headed by Paul Duffen in June 2007.

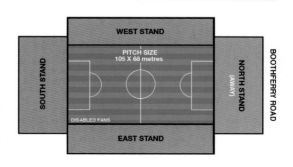

1 A1105 Anlaby Road
2 Arnold Lane
3 West Stand
4 East Stand
5 Walton Street
6 To city centre and railway station
7 Car parks
8 Railway line towards Scarborough
9 Railway line towards Leeds
10 A1105 westwards towards A63 and M62

↘ North direction (approx)

◂ 700568
▾ 700578

Ipswich Town

Portman Road
Ipswich, IP1 2DA

Tel No: 01473 400500

Advance Tickets Tel No: 0870 1110555

Fax: 01473 400040

Web Site: www.itfc.premiumtv.co.uk

E-Mail: enquiries@itfc.co.uk

League: League Championship

Last Season: 14th (P 46; W 18; D 8; L 20; GF 64; GA 59)

Training Ground: Ipswich Town Academy, Playford Road, Rushmere, Ipswich IP4 5RU

Nickname: Tractorboys

Brief History: Founded 1887 as Ipswich Association F.C., changed to Ipswich Town in 1888. Former Grounds: Broom Hill & Brookes Hall, moved to Portman Road in 1888. Record attendance 38,010

(Total) Current Capacity: 30,311 all seated

Visiting Supporters' Allocation: 1,700 all seated in Cobbold Stand

Club Colours: Blue shirts, white shorts

Nearest Railway Station: Ipswich

Parking (Car): Portman Road, Portman Walk & West End Road

Parking (Coach/Bus): West End Road

Police Force and Tel No: Suffolk (01473 611611)

Disabled Visitors' Facilities:
Wheelchairs: Lower Britannia Stand
Blind: Commentary available

Anticipated Development(s): The new Greene King (South) Stand has been followed by the construction of the new two-tier, 7,035-seat, North Stand, which was initially delayed as a result of legal action. The completion of the two stands takes Portman Road's capacity to more than 30,000.

One of a number of erstwhile Premier League teams that are struggling to adjust to life in the Championship, Jim Magilton's Ipswich Town side struggled to make an impact at this level although in finishing 14th the team did marginally better on its showing in 2005/06. For teams such as Ipswich, the real problem is that the relegated teams from the Premier League have the benefit of the parachute payments for two years whilst there are also a number of other Championship teams that have received additional funding. This makes competing for Town ever more difficult and thus a serious promotion push almost impossible. In addition to struggling in the league, the Tractorboys also had a disappointing exit from the Carling Cup, losing on penalties in the first round away at League Two Peterborough United. For 2007/08 a top-half finish should be possible but with 11 points covering 12th to 18th position in 2006/07 a few bad results could see a dramatic fall down the table.

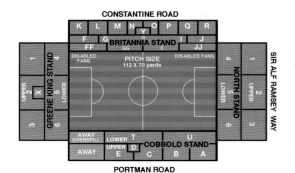

C Club Offices
E Entrance(s) for visiting supporters
R Refreshment bars for visiting supporters
T Toilets for visiting supporters

1 A137 West End Road
2 Sir Alf Ramsay Way
3 Portman Road
4 Princes Street
5 To Ipswich BR Station
6 Car Parks
7 Cobbold Stand
8 Britannia Stand
9 North Stand
10 Greene King (South) Stand

↘ North direction (approx)

◄ 699778
▼ 699784

Leeds United

Elland Road
Leeds, LS11 0ES

Tel No: 0113 367 6000

Advance Tickets Tel No: 0871 334 1992

Fax: 0113 367 6050

Web Site: www.leedsunited.com

E-mail: reception@leedsunited.com

League: League Two

Last Season: 24th (relegated; 10 points deducted
for going into Administration)
(P 46; W 13; D 7; L 26; GF 46; GA 72)

Training Ground: Thorp Arch, Walton Road, Nr
Wetherby LS23 7BA

Nickname: United

Brief History: Founded 1919, formed from the
former 'Leeds City' Club, who were
disbanded following expulsion from the
Football League in October 1919. Joined
Football League in 1920. Record attendance
57,892

(Total) Current Capacity: 40,296 (all seated)

Visiting Supporters' Allocation: 1,725 in South
East Corner (can be increased to 3,662 in
South Stand if necessary)

Club Colours: White shirts, white shorts

Nearest Railway Station: Leeds City

Parking (Car): Car parks adjacent to ground

Parking (Coach/Bus): As directed by Police

Police Force and Tel No: West Yorkshire (0113
243 5353)

Disabled Visitors' Facilities:
Wheelchairs: West Stand and South Stand
Blind: Commentary available

Anticipated Development(s): Although the
club had proposals for relocation to a new
50,000-seat stadium costing £60 million to be
constructed close to the A1/M1 link road,
given the club's high profile financial
problems and recent relegation to League
Two, it is unclear whether this work will
proceed. The club has sold the Elland Road
site and leased it back.

Football is a fickle sport. At the end of the 2005/06
season Kevin Blackwell led out his Leeds United team
at the Millennium Stadium in the final of the League
Championship Play-offs. Less than four months later, he's
sacked with his team standing at 23rd in the
Championship although through to the third round of the
Carling Cup. Blackwell had been Leeds' manager for some
two years and had had some success, following the club's
financial problems, in shaping a team capable of making
a challenge in 2005/06 but a poor run of League form,
culminating in a 3-0 home defeat to Sunderland and a 1–0
defeat at Coventry City sealed his fate. John Carver took
over as caretaker manager but his reign was short-lived
and the club appointed Dennis Wise in early November.
Under Wise the club, however, continued to struggle and
relegation to League Two — the first time in the club's
history that it will be playing in the third tier of English
football — was confirmed before the end of the season.
With relegation all but assured, Ken Bates, the club
chairman, put the club into Administration, thereby
guaranteeing that the 10-point deduction would take
effect at the end of the current season and not be carried
through to the start of next year. As other clubs have
discovered, going into Administration can be fraught but,
at the time of writing, it looks as though a new company,
led again by Bates, will ensure the club's future in 2007/08
and beyond. On the field, relegation will inevitably hasten
the departure of the club's leading players, such as David
Healy, and this, combined with the financial constraints
during the period of Administration, will make Wise's job
in putting together a team to challenge for promotion
difficult. Given the circumstances, perhaps a Play-Off place
is the best that the Elland Road faithful can look forward
to.

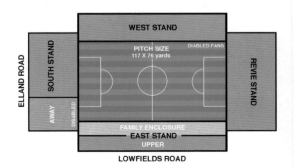

C Club Offices
S Club Shop
E Entrance(s) for visiting
supporters

1 M621
2 M621 Junction 2
3 A643 Elland Road
4 Lowfields Road
5 To A58
6 City Centre and BR station
7 To M62 and M1

↘ North direction (approx)

◄ 700145
▼ 700135

Leicester City

Walkers Stadium
Filbert Way, Leicester, LE2 7FL

Tel No: 0870 040 6000

Advance Tickets Tel No: 0870 499 1884

Fax: 0116 291 1254

Web Site: www.lcfc.premiumtv.co.uk

E-mail: ticket.sales@lcfc.co.uk

League: League Championship

Last Season: 19th
(P46; W 13; D 14; L 19; GF 49; GA 64)

Training Ground: Belvoir Drive, Leicester LE2 8PB

Nickname: The Foxes

Brief History: Founded 1884 as Leicester Fosse, changed name to Leicester City in 1919. Former grounds: Fosse Road South, Victoria Road, Belgrave Cycle Track, Mill Lane, Aylstone Road Cricket Ground and Filbert Street (from 1891). The club moved to the new Walkers Stadium for the start of the 2002/03 season. Record attendance (at Filbert Street) 47,298; (at Walkers Stadium) 32,148

(Total) Current Capacity: 32,500

Visiting Supporters' Allocation: 3,000 (all seated) in North East of Ground

Club Colours: Blue shirts, white shorts

Nearest Railway Station: Leicester

Parking (Car): NCP car park

Parking (Coach/Bus): As directed

Police Force and Tel No: Leicester (0116 222 2222)

Disabled Visitors Facilities:

Wheelchairs: 186 spaces spread through all stands

Blind: Match commentary via hospital radio

Anticipated Developments: The club moved into the new 32,500-seat Walkers Stadium at the start of the 2002/03 season. Although there are no plans at present, the stadium design allows for the construction of a second tier to the East Stand, taking capacity to 40,000.

Taken over during the course of the season by ex-Portsmouth chairman, Milan Mandaric, it was always likely that there were going to be changes at the Walkers Stadium. One of the casualties was manager Rob Kelly, who was dismissed just after Easter following a 3-0 defeat at Plymouth. The result, the Foxes' eighth match without a win, left the team just five points above the Championship drop-zone at a time when the teams below them were starting to pick up points. The club moved quickly to appoint ex-Norwich boss Nigel Worthington as manager until the end of the season. However, under Worthington, the team continued to struggle and ultimately finishing in 19th position, effectively only seven points above the drop zone was a disappointment. After the end of the season it was announced that ex-Milton Keynes Dons' boss Martin Allen would be taking over as manager for the 2007/08 season. Allen, whose teams have a reputation for playing direct football, has had success in the past couple of seasons in taking both Brentford and Milton Keynes into Play-Offs, will undoubtedly produce an effective team but whether it will have the sophistication to compete at League Championship level remains to be seen. The club should improve on its 19th place but a top-half finish is perhaps the best estimate for 2007/08.

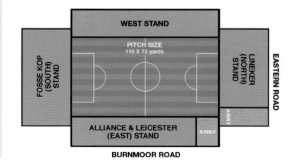

C Club Offices

1 Raw Dykes Road
2 Eastern Road
3 A426 Aylestone Road
4 To Lutterworth
5 To city centre and railway station (one mile)
6 Burnmoor Street
7 River Soar

↘ North direction (approx)

◄ 699793
▼ 699804

Leyton Orient

Matchroom Stadium
Brisbane Road, Leyton, London, E10 5NF

Tel No: 020 8926 1111

Advance Tickets Tel No: 020 8926 1010

Fax: 020 8926 1110

Web Site: www.leytonorient.premiumtv.co.uk

E-Mail: info@leytonorient.net

League: League One

Last Season: 20th
(P 46; W 12; D 15; L 19; GF 61; GA 77)

Training Ground: Southgate Hockey Centre, Trent Park, Snakes Lane, Barnet EN4 0PS

Nickname: The O's

Brief History: Founded 1887 as Clapton Orient, from Eagle Cricket Club (formerly Glyn Cricket Club formed in 1881). Changed name to Leyton Orient (1946), Orient (1966), Leyton Orient (1987). Former grounds: Glyn Road, Whittles Athletic Ground, Millfields Road, Lea Bridge Road, Wembley Stadium (2 games), moved to Brisbane Road in 1937. Record attendance 34,345

(Total) Current Capacity: 9,271 (all-seated)

Visiting Supporters' Allocation: 1,000 (all seated) in East Stand/Terrace

Club Colours: Red shirts, red shorts

Nearest Railway Station: Leyton (tube), Leyton Midland Road

Parking (Car): Street parking

Parking (Coach/Bus): As directed by Police

Police Force and Tel No: Metropolitan (020 8556 8855)

Disabled Visitors' Facilities:
Wheelchairs: Windsor Road
Blind: Match commentary supplied on request

Anticipated Development(s): The club's plans to construct a new 1,300-seat stand on the north side of the ground received a major set-back in October when the plans for the development were rejected by the London Borough of Waltham Forest. The club intended to appeal against the decision and finally obtained planning permission in early January. Work was scheduled to start on the stand towards the end of the month and the new 1,351-seat structure was completed by the end of the 2006/07 season. Further work will see the construction of 16 flats at the north end of the ground and 46 at the south end.

Promoted at the end of 2005/06, the first season in League One was always going to be a struggle for Martin Ling and his Orient team and undoubtedly the club struggled to make an impact. For the early part of the season it looked as though relegation was all but assured; however, the team did perform well enough — just — to ensure that League One football will again be on offer at Brisbane Road. In terms of a defining match, the 2-0 victory away at fellow strugglers Bradford City was perhaps it; victory for City would have lifted the Yorkshire team away from the drop zone whilst leaving the O's deep in trouble but the victory sapped Bradford's confidence and ensured that the initiative was with Ling's team. During the season, scoring goals was not the team's problem; conceding 77 during the course of the campaign was. Provided that Ling can address the question of his leaky defence in the close season, Orient should do better in 2007/08, although it's hard to escape the conclusion that the club faces another battle against the drop.

C Club Offices
S Club Shop
E Entrance(s) for visiting
   supporters

1 Buckingham Road
2 Oliver Road
3 A112 High Road Leyton
4 To Leyton Tube Station
   (¼ mile)
5 Brisbane Road
6 Windsor Road
7 To Leyton Midland Road
   BR station
8 South Stand
9 West Stand
10 Main (East) Stand
11 North Stand

↘ North direction (approx)

◀ 700935
▼ 700927

Lincoln City

Sincil Bank
Lincoln LN5 8LD

Tel No: 0870 899 2005

Advance Tickets Tel No: 0870 899 2005

Fax: 01522 880020

Web Site: www.redimps.premiumtv.co.uk

E-Mail: lcfc@redimps.com

League: League Two

Last Season: 5th
(P 46; W 21; D 11; L 14; GF 70; GA 59)

Training Ground: The Sports Ground, Carlton Boulevard, Lincoln LN2 4WJ

Nickname: The Imps

Brief History: Founded 1884. Former Ground: John O'Gaunts Ground, moved to Sincil Bank in 1895. Founder-members 2nd Division Football League (1892). Relegated from 4th Division in 1987, promoted from GM Vauxhall Conference in 1988. Record attendance 23,196

(Total) Current Capacity: 10,130 (all seated)

Visiting Supporters' Allocation: 2,000 in Co-op Community Stand (part, remainder for Home fans)

Club Colours: Red and white striped shirts, black shorts

Nearest Railway Station: Lincoln Central

Parking (Car): City centre car parks; limited on-street parking

Parking (Coach/Bus): South Common

Police Force and Tel No: Lincolnshire (01522 529911)

Disabled Visitors' Facilities:
Wheelchairs: The Simons and South (Mundy) Park stands
Blind: No special facility

Anticipated Development(s): Following the replacement of the seats in the Stacey West Stand, Sincil Bank is once again an all-seater stadium.

Another season, another flirtation with the Play-Offs. Yet another failure to achieve promotion. In a season where League Two was dominated by the four teams relegated from League One at the end of the 2005/06 season, John Schofield's team finished a creditable fifth as best of the also-rans, although this was no less than 10 points below Milton Keynes in fourth. Thus, once again, City's season was extended by competition in the Play-Offs, where the team faced an in-form Bristol Rovers over two legs. The West Country team, however, proved too strong, winning 2-1 at home and defeating the Imps 5-3 at Sincil Bank. Thus, once again, League Two football will again be on offer for Lincoln fans and, if the pattern of 2006/07 is repeated in terms of the strength of the relegated teams, then a Play-Off place may again be the best that the Imps can look forward to.

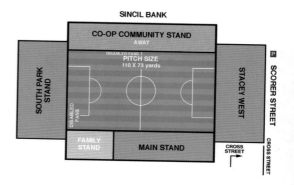

C Club Offices
S Club Shop
E Entrance(s) for visiting supporters

1 Family Stand
2 Sincil Bank
3 Sausthorpe Street
4 Cross Street
5 Co-op Community Stand (away)
6 A158 South Park Avenue
7 Stacey West Stand
8 Lincoln Central BR Station (½ mile)

↘ North direction (approx)

◄ 700580
▼ 700587

Anfield Road
Liverpool L4 0TH

Tel No: 0151 263 2361
Advance Tickets Tel No: 0870 220 2345
Fax: 0151 260 8813
Ticket Enquiries Fax: 0151 261 1416
Web Site: www.liverpoolfc.tv
League: F.A. Premier
Last Season: 3rd
(P 38; W 20; D 7; L 10; GF 55; GA 25)
Training Ground: Melwood Drive, West Derby, Liverpool L12 8SV; Tel: 0151 282 8888
Nickname: The Reds
Brief History: Founded 1892. Anfield Ground formerly Everton F.C. Ground. Joined Football League in 1893. Record attendance 61,905
(Total) Current Capacity: 45,362 (all seated)
Visiting Supporters' Allocation: 1,972 (all seated) in Anfield Road Stand
Club Colours: Red shirts, red shorts
Nearest Railway Station: Kirkdale
Parking (Car): Stanley car park
Parking (Coach/Bus): Priory Road and Pinehurst Avenue
Police Force and Tel No: Merseyside (0151 709 6010)
Disabled Visitors' Facilities:
Wheelchairs: Kop and Main Stands
Blind: Commentary available
Anticipated Development(s): The plans for the club's relocation received a boost in September 2006 when the council agreed to grant the club a 999-year lease on part of Stanley Park. The new ground, to be located some 300yd from Anfield, is scheduled to be completed for the start of the 2010/11 season and will cost some £210 million for a ground with a 60,000-seat capacity. Later in September it was announced that European funding for the associated redevelopment scheme of the Stanley Park area — a requirement of the planning permission — had also been secured; this funding allows the club to access funds from the council and the Development Agency again to part fund this work. During the 2006/07 season, the club was acquired by two Americans; as part of their post-takeover review, the two are looking at the possibility of expanding the size of the new ground although, in the meantime, work on the existing project continues.

There was a distinct feeling of change at Anfield during the season, with the sale of the club to two American businessmen as Liverpool became one of a number of clubs to fall into foreign ownership during the course of the season. On the field, Liverpool maintained its position as being one of the more serious challengers to the dominance of the Premier League by Manchester United and Chelsea, although fishing more than 20 points adrift of the eventual champions is an indication of the magnitude of the task facing Rafael Benitez if he is going to turn Liverpool into serious title contenders in 2007/08. Apart from the league, the team also had more success in Europe, reaching the final of the Champions League courtesy of a semi-final victory over Chelsea. Facing AC Milan again, this time in Athens, the boot was on the other foot this year with the Italian team ultimately winning 2-1 despite Liverpool dominating much of the play. After the match, Benitez made pertinent comments about the scale of the investment required if Liverpool were to achieve domestic success. With new money from TV rights to look forward to and with the backing of the club's new owners, it's likely that Liverpool will enter the new season considerably strengthened. If that's the case then the club ought to be able to sustain a serious challenge for the title but the reality may well be that the club's best route for more silverware will again come through one of the cup competitions.

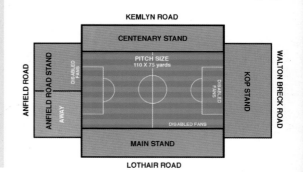

C Club Offices
S Club Shop

1 Car Park
2 Anfield Road
3 A5089 Walton Breck Road
4 Kemlyn Road
5 Kirkdale BR Station
  (1 mile)
6 Utting Avenue
7 Stanley Park
8 Spion Kop
9 Anfield Road Stand

↖ North direction (approx)

◀ 700015
▼ 700030

Luton Town

Kenilworth Road Stadium
1 Maple Road, Luton, LU4 8AW

Tel No: 01582 411622

Advance Tickets Tel No: 01582 416976

Fax: 01582 405070

Web Site: www.lutontown.premiumtv.co.uk

E-Mail: clubsec@lutontown.co.uk

League: League One

Last Season: 23rd (relegated)
(P 46; W 10; D 10; L 26; GF 53; GA 81)

Training Ground: Woolham's Playing Fields,
Harpenden Road, St Albans

Nickname: The Hatters

Brief History: Founded 1885 from an
amalgamation of Wanderers F.C. and
Excelsior F.C. Former Grounds: Dallow Lane &
Dunstable Road, moved to Kenilworth Road
in 1905. Record attendance 30,069

(Total) Current Capacity: 9,970 (all seated)

Visiting Supporters' Allocation: 2,200

Club Colours: White shirts,
black shorts

Nearest Railway Station: Luton

Parking (Car): Street parking

Parking (Coach/Bus): Luton bus station

Police Force and Tel No: Bedfordshire (01582
401212)

Disabled Visitors' Facilities:
Wheelchairs: Kenilworth Road and Main
stands
Blind: Commentary available

Anticipated Development(s): One of a number
of clubs to enter Administration following
the collapse of ITV Digital, in the summer of
2004 it was announced that the new
consortium hoping to take-over the club still
intended to relocate, but there is still no
definite timescale. A new owner, David
Pinkney, was confirmed during July 2007; he
reaffirmed the intention that the club was
still planning to relocate to a new 25,000-
seat stadium although there is no confirmed
time-frame.

A turbulent season at Kenilworth Road seemed
to have started reasonably well with the team
challenging for a Play-Off place but, following the sale
of a number of key players in the January transfer
window, form collapsed and, by the middle of March
with Town firmly ensconced in the relegation zone,
Mike Newell — who'd had his own problems during
the year, most notably comments regarding female
match officials — was sacked as manager. He was
replaced as caretaker by ex-player Brian Stein before
the appointment of ex-Leeds boss Kevin Blackwell in
late March. Ironically, the only team below Luton at
the time of Blackwell's appointment was Leeds United.
Blackwell, however, was unable to arrest Town's
decline and relegation was confirmed well before the
end of the season. However, as a result of Leeds
entering Administration with the consequent 10-point
deduction, Town did not finish bottom of the
Championship. As a relegated team, the Hatters
should have the potential to make a serious challenge
for promotion back into the Championship, but with a
number of other ambitious teams in League One —
such as Nottingham Forest — it may well be that the
team's best route to promotion will be through the
Play-Offs.

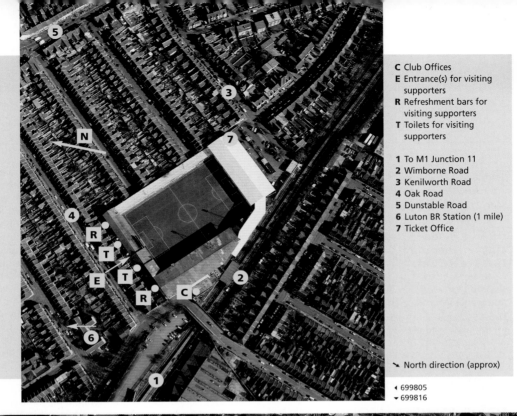

C Club Offices
E Entrance(s) for visiting supporters
R Refreshment bars for visiting supporters
T Toilets for visiting supporters

1 To M1 Junction 11
2 Wimborne Road
3 Kenilworth Road
4 Oak Road
5 Dunstable Road
6 Luton BR Station (1 mile)
7 Ticket Office

North direction (approx)

◀ 699805
▼ 699816

Macclesfield Town

Moss Rose Ground
London Road, Macclesfield, SK11 7SP

Tel No: 01625 264686
Advance Tickets Tel No: 01625 264686
Fax: 01625 264692
Web Site: www.mtfc.premiumtv.co.uk
E-Mail: office@mtfc.co.uk
League: League Two
Last Season: 22nd
(P 46; W 12; D 12; L 22; GF 55; GA 77)
Training Ground: No current facility
Nickname: The Silkmen
Brief History: Founded 1874. Previous ground: Rostron Field moved to Moss Rose Ground in 1891. Winners of the Vauxhall Conference in 1994/95 and 1997/97. Admitted to Football League for 1997/98 season. Record attendance 10,041
(Total) Current Capacity: 6,335 (2,599 seated)
Visiting Supporters' Allocation: 1,900 (1,500 in Silkman Terrace; 400 seated in Estate Road Stand)
Club Colours: Royal blue, royal blue shorts
Nearest Railway Station: Macclesfield
Parking (Car): No parking at the ground and the nearest off-street car park is in the town centre (25min walk). There is some on-street parking in the vicinity, but this can get crowded.
Parking (Coach/Bus): As directed
Police Force and Tel No: Cheshire (01625 610000)
Disabled Visitors' Facilities:
Wheelchairs: 45 places in Estate Road Stand
Blind: No special facility
Anticipated Development(s): The new Estate Road (Alfred McAlpine) Stand, with its 1,497 seats, was completed towards the end of the 2000/01 season and officially opened on 5 May 2001. This is the first phase of a scheme to redevelop Moss Rose; the next phase will see a seated second tier raised above the existing terrace at the Silkman End. Other recent work has included the provision of permanent toilets at the away end.

Following a disastrous start to the season with no wins in the club's first 12 league matches, a sequence which left the club in 24th place already eight points adrift, Brian Horton was sacked as manager in early October. Player-coach Ian Brightwell took over as caretaker before the inspired appointment of Paul Ince. Under Ince the club's playing fortunes improved immeasurably with the moving from basket case, where relegation seemed well nigh certain, to a position where League Two safety was achievable. However, a couple of poor results towards the end of the campaign threatened to undermine all the good work that Ince had done. On the last day of the season, three clubs — Boston, Macclesfield and Wrexham — all faced the drop. A home draw against Notts County was sufficient to keep the Silkmen up, although fans at Moss Rose must have feared the worse when Boston went into the lead at Wrexham. For 2007/08 fans will be hoping for a much better start to the season — there's little purpose in giving the competition a massive advantage — and that the form of the second half of the 2006/07 campaign can be replicated. If that's the case then a top-half finish is by no means impossible. However, with the departure of Paul Ince, confirmed at the end of June, the new manager (still to be confirmed at the time of writing), will have his work cut out.

A523 LONDON ROAD

C Club Offices
E Entrance(s) for visiting
supporters

1 A523 London Road
2 To Town Centre and BR
station (1.5 miles)
3 To Leek
4 Moss Lane
5 Star Lane
6 Site of Silkmans Public
House (now demolished)
7 Star Lane End
8 Silkman End (away
section)
9 Estate Road Stand

↘ North direction (approx)

◄ 700602
▼ 700598

The City of Manchester Stadium
Sportcity, Manchester M11 3FF

Tel No: 0870 062 1894

Advance Tickets Tel No: 0870 062 1894

Fax: 0161 438 7999

Web Site: www.mcfc.co.uk

E-mail: mcfc@mcfc.co.uk

League: F.A. Premier

Last Season: 14th
(P 38; W 11; D 9; L 18; GF 29; GA 44)

Training Ground: Platt Lane Complex, Yew Tree Road, Fallowfield, Manchester M14 7UU; Tel: 0161 248 6610; Fax: 0161 257 0030

Nickname: The Blues

Brief History: Founded 1880 at West Gorton, changed name to Ardwick (reformed 1887) and to Manchester City in 1894. Former grounds: Clowes Street (1880-81), Kirkmanshulme Cricket Club (1881-82), Queens Road (1882-84), Pink Bank Lane (1884-87), Hyde Road (1887-1923) and Maine Road (from 1923 until 2003). Moved to the City of Manchester Stadium for the start of the 2003/04 season. Founder-members 2nd Division (1892). Record attendance (at Maine Road) 84,569 (record for a Football League Ground); at City of Manchester Stadium 47,304

(Total) Current Capacity: 48,000

Visiting Supporters' Allocation: 3,000 (South Stand); can be increased to 4,500 if required

Club Colours: Sky blue shirts, white shorts

Nearest Railway Station: Manchester Piccadilly

Parking (Car): Ample match day parking available to the north of the stadium, entrance via Alan Turing Way. On-street parking restrictions operate in all areas adjacent to the stadium on matchdays.

Parking (Coach/Bus): Coach parking for visiting supporters is adjacent to turnstiles at Key 103 Stand. For home supporters to the north of the stadium, entrance from Alan Turing Way.

Police Force and Tel No: Greater Manchester (0161 872 5050)

Disabled Visitors' facilities:
Wheelchairs: 300 disabled seats around ground
Blind: 14 places alongside helpers in East Stand Level 1. Commentary available via headsets.

A hugely disappointing season at Eastlands saw manager Stuart Pearce dismissed following the end of the campaign with his final game in charge being the 2-1 defeat away at Tottenham Hotspur. Ironically, for a club that might well have been threatened with relegation, in finishing 14th the team actually finished higher than in 2006/07. If there was one major problem for the team during the season it was goals — no more than 10 were scored at home in the league and only 19 away. Fortunately, however, as one would expect from a team managed by Pearce, the defence was mean with only 44 goals conceded. With an average of less than two goals a game, watching City play during the 2006/07 season must have been the footballing equivalent of purgatory! Even in cup competitions, City struggled losing 2-1 away at League One outfit Chesterfield in the second round of the Carling Cup. Apart from the departure of Pearce, there was further uncertainty at the club over its on-off sale to the ex-Thai Prime Minister Thaksin Shinawatra and over Pearce's successor. owards the end of June it was confirmed that Shinawatra's take-over was progressing and that ex-England boss Sven-Goran Eriksson was confirmed as the new team manager. Although Eriksson's tenure as national coach was not without controversy, he had proved himself an astute manager at club level before the appointment and he should be able to attract quality players to City as a result, particularly if the new owner delivers the additional funding required for strengthening the squad. It promises to be an interesting season for the blue half of Manchester!

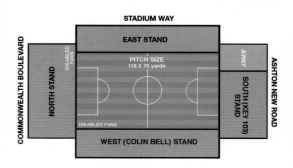

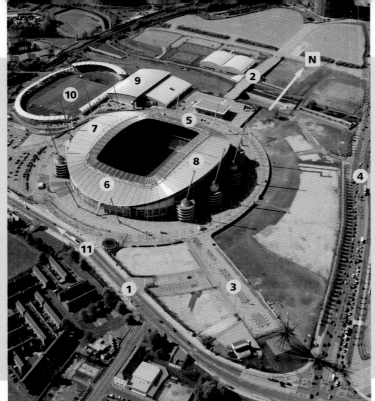

1 A662 Ashton New Road
2 Commonwealth Boulevard
3 Stadium Way
4 A6010 Alan Turing Way
5 North Stand
6 South (Key 103) Stand
7 West (Colin Bell) Stand
8 East Stand
9 National Squash Centre
10 Warm-up track
11 To Manchester city centre and Piccadilly station (1.5 miles)

↘ North direction (approx)

◀ 700078
▼ 700072

Old Trafford
Sir Matt Busby Way, Manchester, M16 0RA

Tel No: 0161 868 8000

Advance Tickets Tel No: 0870 442 1999

Fax: 0161 868 8804

Web Site: www.manutd.com

E-mail: enquiries@manutd.co.uk

League: F.A. Premier

Last Season: 1st
(P 38; W 28; D 5; L 5; GF 83; GA 27)

Training Ground: Carrington Training Complex, Birch Road, Manchester M31 4HH

Nickname: The Red Devils

Brief History: Founded in 1878 as 'Newton Heath L&Y', later Newton Heath, changed to Manchester United in 1902. Former Grounds: North Road, Monsall & Bank Street, Clayton, moved to Old Trafford in 1910 (used Manchester City F.C. Ground 1941-49). Founder-members Second Division (1892). Record attendance 76,962.

(Total) Current Capacity: 76,100 (all seated)

Visiting Supporters' Allocation: Approx. 3,000 in corner of South and East Stands

Club Colours: Red shirts, white shorts

Nearest Railway Station: At Ground

Parking (Car): Lancashire Cricket Ground and White City

Parking (Coach/Bus): As directed by Police

Police Force and Tel No: Greater Manchester (0161 872 5050)

Disabled Visitors' Facilities:
Wheelchairs: South East Stand
Blind: Commentary available

Anticipated Development(s): The work on the £45 million project construct infills at the north-east and north-west corners of the ground has now been completed and takes Old Trafford's capacity to 76,000, making it by some margin the largest league ground in Britain. Any future development of the ground will involve the Main (South) stand although work here is complicated by the proximity of the building to the adjacent railway line.

After a couple of seasons where United saw the title won at a canter by Chelsea, the 2006/07 season saw the Premier League title head, once again, to Old Trafford. At the start of the season, there was concern that two of the club's stars — Wayne Rooney and Christiano Ronaldo — would find it difficult to play together as a result of the fall-out following Rooney's sending-off in the World Cup quarter final against Portugal and, whilst Ronaldo undoubtedly got harsh treatment from opposing fans, on the field the two achieved much, including Goal of the Season. With the Premier League title looking like a two-horse race for much of the season, United had the Championship sewn up before the anticipated decider at Stamford Bridge. Away from the league, however, Ferguson's team did suffer the embarrassment of a 1-0 defeat away at Southend United in the fourth round of the Carling Cup and the disappointment of defeat by Chelsea in a poor FA Cup final. The biggest disappointment was probably the defeat in the Champions League semi-final by AC Milan following the crushing of Roma in the quarter-finals. With the club making significant signings during the close season — with Portuguese winger Nani and Brazilian Anderson already on the books — United will go into 2007/08 even stronger. Domestically, they will undoubtedly again be the team to beat in any competition but the challenge for Ferguson will, once again, be to convert this dominance into a serious challenge for the Champions League.

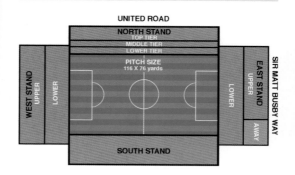

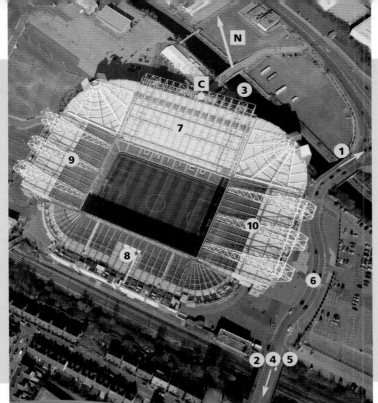

C Club Offices

1 To A5081 Trafford Park Road to M63 Junction 4 (5 miles)
2 A56 Chester Road
3 Bridgewater Canal
4 To Old Trafford Cricket Ground
5 To Parking and Warwick Road BR Station
6 Sir Matt Busby Way
7 North Stand
8 South Stand
9 West Stand
10 East Stand

↘ North direction (approx)

◄ 700640
▼ 700649

Mansfield Town

Field Mill Stadium
Quarry Lane, Mansfield, Notts, NG18 5DA

Tel No: 0870 756 3160

Advance Tickets Tel No: 0870 756 3160

Fax: 01623 482495

Web Site: www.mansfieldtown.premiumtv.co.uk

E-mail: stags@stags.plus.com

League: League Two

Last Season: 17th
(P46; W 14; D 12; L 20; GF 58; GA 63)

Training Ground: The John Fretwell Sports Complex, Sookholme Road, Sookholme, Mansfield NG19 8LL

Nickname: The Stags

Brief History: Founded 1910 as Mansfield Wesleyans Boys Brigade, changed to Mansfield Town in 1914. Former Grounds: Pelham Street, Newgate Lane and The Prairie, moved to Field Mill in 1919. Record attendance 24,467

(Total) Current Capacity: 9,990 (all seated)

Visiting Supporters' Allocation: 1,800 (all seated) in North Stand

Club Colours: Amber with blue trim shirts, Blue shorts with amber trim

Nearest Railway Station: Mansfield

Parking (Car): Car park at Ground

Parking (Coach/Bus): Car park at Ground

Police Force and Tel No: Nottinghamshire (01623 420999)

Disabled Visitors' Facilities:
Wheelchairs: Facilities provided in North, West and South stands
Blind: No special facility

Anticipated Development(s): Work on the Main Stand and on the North and Quarry Lane ends was completed in early 2001, leaving the Bishop Street Stand as the only unreconstructed part of Field Mill. Plans exist for this to be rebuilt as a 2,800-seat structure but the time scale is unconfirmed.

An unwelcome early Christmas present arrived for Peter Shirtliff when, following a run of one victory in eight games, he was sacked as manager of the Stags after some 15 months in the job. Assistant boss, Paul Holland, took over as caretaker with the club in 18th position, four points above the drop zone. The club moved quickly to appoint ex-boss Billy Dearden, who had previously been in charge between June 1999 and January 2002, as new boss until the end of the season. Under Dearden, the club's playing fortunes picked up with the club reaching the dizzy heights of 12th place and a sniff of the Play-Offs — Shrewsbury were 11th at this stage and did reach seventh place — before a poor run of form — only one win in the last 10 league games – saw the Stags drop back down the table. Unless there is a dramatic pick-up in form early in the 2007/08 season, it's likely that Town will again be battling at the wrong end of the League Two table.

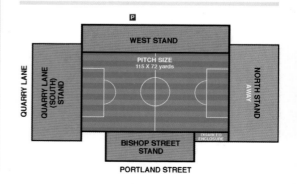

E Entrance(s) for visiting supporters

1 Car Park(s)
2 Quarry Lane
3 A60 Nottingham Road to M1 Junction 27
4 Portland Street
5 To A38 and M1 Junction 28
6 To Town Centre
7 Mansfield railway station
8 North Stand (away)
9 Quarry Lane End (South Stand)
10 Bishop Street Stand
11 Main (West) Stand

↘ North direction (approx)

◀ 700605
▾ 700611

Middlesbrough

Riverside Stadium
Middlesbrough, Cleveland TS3 6RS

Tel No: 0844 499 6789

Advance Tickets Tel No: 0844 499 1234

Fax: 01642 757690

Web Site: www.mfc.co.uk

E-mail: enquiries@mfc.co.uk

League: F.A. Premier

Last Season: 12th
(P 38; W 12; D 10; L 16; GF 44; GA 49)

Training Ground: Rockcliffe Park, Hurworth Place, Near Darlington, County Durham DL2 2DU; Tel: 01325 722222

Nickname: Boro

Brief History: Founded 1876. Former Grounds: Archery Ground (Albert Park), Breckon Hill Road, Linthorpe Road, moved to Ayresome Park in 1903, and to current ground in Summer 1995. F.A. Amateur Cup winners 1894 and 1897 (joined Football League in 1899). Record attendance (Ayresome Park) 53,596, (Riverside Stadium) 35,000

(Total) Current Capacity: 35,100 (all seated)

Visiting Supporters' Allocation: 3,450 (in the South Stand)

Club Colours: Red shirts, red shorts

Nearest Railway Station: Middlesbrough

Parking (Car): All parking at stadium is for permit holders

Parking (Coach/Bus): As directed

Police Force and Tel No: Cleveland (01642 248184)

Disabled Visitors' Facilities:
Wheelchairs: More than 170 places available for disabled fans
Blind: Commentary available

Anticipated Development(s): There remain long term plans for the ground's capacity to be increased to 42,000 through the construction of extra tiers on the North, South and East stands, although there is no confirmed timetable for this work at the current time.

Having a tyro manager in Gareth Southgate always meant that the season had the potential to be a tough one at the Riverside Stadium and there must have been occasions during the campaign when Southgate wondered whether he'd made the right decision. Such concerns must have been heightened by results such as the 2-0 home defeat by Notts County in the second round of the Carling Cup. In the league, the team hovered just above the drop zone for much of the campaign, ultimately finishing in 12th place eight points above relegated Sheffield United. With a number of key players, such as Yakubu, Viduka and Schwarzer probably departing from the Riverside during the close season, much will depend on the quality of the players that Southgate is able to recruit. With the big clubs gaining significant investment either from new owners or from enlarged grounds it is increasingly difficult for a middling Premier League team such as Boro to make a sustained challenge for a top-seven position but it is also very easy, with a few bad results, to end up in the battle to avoid the drop. Chairman Steve Gibson has, over the years, proved to be loyal to his managers but another mid-table position is perhaps the best that he and the Boro faithful can look forward to in 2007/08.

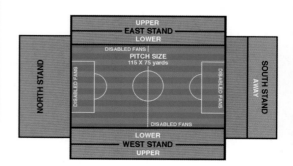

C Club Offices
S Club Shop
1 Cargo Fleet Road
2 To Middlesbrough railway station
3 To Middlesbrough town centre
4 Middlesbrough Docks
5 Shepherdson Way to A66
6 South Stand
7 Car parks

↖ North direction (approx)

◄ 700621
▼ 700627

Millwall

New Den
Bolina Road, London, SE16 3LN

Tel No: 020 7232 1222

Advance Tickets Tel No: 020 7231 9999

Fax: 020 7231 3663

Web Site: www.millwallfc.premiumtv.co.uk

E-mail: questions@millwallplc.com

League: League One

Last Season: 10th
(P 46; W 19; D 9; L 18; GF 59; GA 62)

Training Ground: Millwall FC Training Ground, Calmont Road (off Ashgrove Road), Bromley Hill, Bromley, Kent BR1 4BZ

Nickname: The Lions

Brief History: Founded 1885 as Millwall Rovers, changed name to Millwall Athletic (1889) and Millwall (1925). Former Grounds: Glengall Road, East Ferry Road (2 separate Grounds), North Greenwich Ground and The Den – Cold Blow Lane – moved to New Den 1993/94 season. Founder-members Third Division (1920). Record attendance (at The Den) 48,672 (at New Den) 20,093

(Total) Current Capacity: 20,150 (all seated)

Visiting Supporters' Allocation: 4,382 in North Stand

Club Colours: Blue shirts, white shorts

Nearest Railway Station: South Bermondsey or Surrey Docks (Tube)

Parking (Car): Juno Way car parking (8 mins walk)

Parking (Coach/Bus): At Ground

Police Force and Tel No: Metropolitan (0207 679 9217)

Disabled Visitors' Facilities:
Wheelchairs: 200 spaces in West Stand Lower Tier
Blind: Commentary available

Towards the end of September, following a run of five defeats that left the team in the drop zone, Nigel Spackman was dismissed as Millwall manager after less than five months in the job. He was replaced as caretaker by his assistant, Willie Donachie. Under Donachie's control, Millwall's form improved immeasurably and, had the season gone on for a couple more weeks then the team may well have been pushing for a Play-Off place. As it was, following the poor start, the team still achieved a top-ten finish, albeit nine points adrift of the all-important sixth place. Provided that the team maintains the form that it showed following the appointment of Donachie, then the Lions could be making a serious bid to reclaim a place in the Championship in the 2007/08 season.

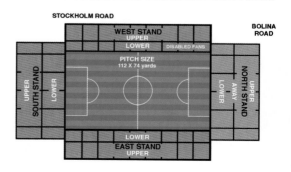

C Club Offices
S Club Shop
E Entrance(s) for visiting
  supporters

1 Bolina Road
2 South Bermondsey station
3 Footpath to station for
  away fans
4 Zampa Road
5 Stockholm Road
6 North Stand (away)

↘ North direction (approx)

◀ 697379
▼ 697384

MK Stadium
Denbigh, Milton Keynes, MK1 1SA

Telephone: 0908 607090*
Advance Tickets Tel No: 01908 609000*
Fax: 01908 209449*
* These are the numbers for the National Hockey Stadium and may well change when the club moves
Web Site: www.mkdons.premiumtv.co.uk
E-mail: info@mkdons.co.uk
League: League Two
Last Season: 4th
(P 46; W 25; D 9; L 12; GF 76; GA 58)
Nickname: The Dons
Brief History: Founded 1889 as Wimbledon Old Centrals, changed name to Wimbledon in 1905 and to Milton Keynes Dons in 2004. Former grounds: Wimbledon Common, Pepy's Road, Grand Drive, Merton Hall Road, Malden Wanderers Cricket Ground, Plough Lane, Selhurst Park (1991-2002) and National Hockey Stadium (2002-2007); moved to Stadium: MK for start of the 2007/08 season. Elected to the Football League in 1997. Record attendance (Plough Lane) 18,000; (Selhurst Park) 30,115; (National Hockey Stadium) 5,306
(Total) Current Capacity: 22,000 (all-seated)
Visiting Supporters' Allocation: tbc
Club Colours: white shirts, white shorts
Nearest Railway Station: Bletchley (two miles); Milton Keynes Central (four miles)
Parking (Car): The ground is located with a retail development and parking restrictions at the ground will probably apply
Parking (Coach/Bus): As directed
Police Force and Tel No: Thames Valley Police (01865 846000)
Disabled Visitors' Facilities:
Wheelchairs: tbc
Blind: tbc
Anticipated Development(s): Following a number of years at the National Hockey Stadium, the Milton Keynes Dons moved into the new Stadium: MK for the start of the 2007/08 season. The ground has been designed to facilitate the addition of a second tier of searing if required in the future, taking the total capacity to 30,000.

In the club's final season at the National Hockey stadium before the move to the new ground, Milton Keynes Dons were in with a mathematic shout for automatic promotion right until the last day of the season as all four teams relegated at the end of 2005/06 battled for the three automatic promotion places. Unfortunately, for Dons' fans, results on the last day — with Swindon achieving a 1-1 draw — meant that the Dons faced Shrewsbury Town in the Play-Offs. In the semi-final, a 0-0 draw at the Gay Meadow — the last game to be played at that venerable ground — seemed to have passed the initiative to Martin Allen's team but, defeat 2-1 in the last game to be played at the National Hockey Stadium consigned the Dons to a further season in League Two. Away from the league, the club had success in the Carling Cup, defeating Championship side Barnsley 2-1 at Oakwell in the second round having beaten another Championship side, Colchester United, at home 1-0 in the first round. After the end of the season it was announced that Allen was leaving to take over at Leicester City. The new manager, still to be confirmed at the time of writing, will take over a club with a new ground and the optimism that this will engender. He will, however, also face the loss of both players and backroom staff. Having been one of the dominant four in 2006/07, Milton Keynes Dons should have the potential to be close to a Play-Off place in 2007/08.

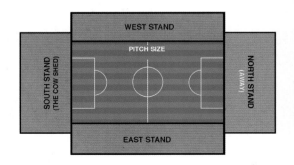

1 B4034 Saxon Street
2 A5
3 Grafton Street
4 Bletcham Way
5 Denbigh Road
6 A5 Southbound to
   London
7 A5 Northbound to
   Milton Keynes centre
   and Towcester
8 To Bletchley railway
   station (two miles)
9 To Milton Keynes
   Central railway station
   (four miles)

↘ North Direction (approx)

◀ 700628
▾ 700638

Christie Park
Lancaster Road, Morecambe, Lancashire LA4 5TJ

Telephone: 01524 411797
Advance Tickets Tel No: 01524 411797
Fax: 01524 832230
Web Site: www.morecambefc.com
E-mail: office@morecambefc.com
League: League Two
Last Season: 3rd (promoted)
(P 46; W 23; D12; L 11; GF 64; GA 46)
Training Ground: New facility being sought for the 2007/08 season
Nickname: Shrimps
Brief History: Founded 1920. Previous grounds: Morecambe Cricket Ground; moved to Roseberry Park 1921; ground later renamed Christie Park after the club's president who had funded its purchase. Joined Conference at the end of the 1995/96 season and promoted to the Football league at the end of the 2006/07 season. Record attendance 9,234
(Total) Current Capacity: 6,400 (1,200 seated)
Visiting Supporters' Allocation: 1,500 (Umbro Stand — all standing) plus limited number of seats in Main Stand
Club Colours: Red shirts, white shorts
Nearest Railway Station: Morecambe
Parking (Car): Main car park is pass only; there is a second small car park otherwise on-street only
Parking (Coach/Bus): As directed
Other clubs sharing ground: Blackburn Reserves
Police Force and Tel No: Lancashire Constabulary (0845 125 3545)
Disabled Visitors' Facilities:
Wheelchairs: 36 home and 10 away spaces
Blind: No special facility
Anticipated Development(s): The club has plans for the reconstruction of the southeast part of the ground. A new three-storey stand, costing £1 million, is scheduled for completion by the start of the 2008/09 season.

One of the longest-surviving members of the Conference — Morecambe — finally achieved promotion to the Football League at the end of the 2006/07 season, when Sammy McIlroy's team finished in third place. In the Play-Off semi-finals, the Shrimps took on one erstwhile League team — York City — drawing 0-0 at Bootham Crescent before winning 1-0 at Christie Park to set up a Wembley visit against another ex-League team in Exeter City. In front of a record crowd for a Conference Play-Off final — 40,043 — Morecambe triumphed 2-1 to enter the Football League for the first time in the club's 87-year history. The new season will be a potentially difficult campaign for Morecambe as the club seeks to adjust to playing at this higher level; recent years have shown that teams promoted through the Conference Play-Offs have occasionally struggled and success for Morecambe may well be simply to ensure League Two survival by the end of the season.

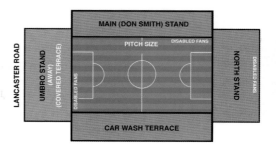

1 B5321 Lancaster Road
2 Lathom Avenue
3 Christie Avenue
4 To Morecambe town centre and railway station (one mile)
5 To A589
6 Ennerdale Avenue
7 Roseberry Avenue
8 Burlington Avenue
9 North Stand
10 Main Stand
11 Umbro Stand (away)
12 Car Wash Terrace

⬊ North direction (approx)

◄ 700865
▼ 700870

Newcastle United

St. James's Park
Newcastle-upon-Tyne, NE1 4ST

Tel No: 0191 201 8400

Advance Tickets Tel No: 0191 261 1571

Fax: 0191 201 8600

Web Site: www.nufc.premiumtv.co.uk

E-mail: custserv@nufc.co.uk

League: F.A. Premier

Last Season: 13th
(P 38; W 11; D 10; L 17; GF 38; GA 47)

Training Ground: Darsley Park, Whitley Road, Benton, Newcastle upon Tyne NE12 9FA

Nickname: The Magpies

Brief History: Founded in 1882 as Newcastle East End, changed to Newcastle United in 1892. Former Grounds: Chillingham Road, moved to St. James' Park (former home of defunct Newcastle West End) in 1892. Record attendance 68,386

(Total) Current Capacity: 52,316 (all seated)

Visiting Supporters' Allocation: 3,000 in North West Stand

Club Colours: Black and white striped shirts, black shorts

Nearest Railway Station: Newcastle Central

Parking (Car): Leazes car park and street parking

Parking (Coach/Bus): Leazes car park

Police Force and Tel No: Northumbria (0191 232 3451)

Disabled Visitors' Facilities:
Wheelchairs: 103 spaces available
Blind: Commentary available

Anticipated Development(s): The club announced plans in March 2007 for a £300 million scheme to increase capacity at St James' Park to 60,000. The work, which would include the construction of a hotel and conference city, will see the expansion of the Gallowgate End. The project, which has yet to receive planning consent, has no confirmed timescale at present.

Another hugely disappointing campaign on Tyneside saw yet another manager disappear through the rotating door at St James's Park with the dismissal of Glenn Roeder, who was replaced by the ex-Bolton boss Sam Allardyce. The pressure seemed to be on Roeder for much of the campaign, his position not being aided by an injury to Michael Owen suffered at the World Cup that kept the England striker out of the team for virtually the entire season, although the team's cup form, particularly in the UEFA Cup, seemed periodically to relieve the pressure. Apart from the change of manager, United is another team to have undergone a change of ownership, although in the case of United, it's a UK-based businessman, Mike Ashley, rather than overseas buyers who has taken over from the Shepherd/Hall regime. With a number of players — notably Owen and Martens — having buy-out clauses in their contracts, Allardyce may well face the prospect of having to rebuild a squad rather than strengthen an existing team. Over recent years, St James's Park has proved to be no respecter of management reputations and with expectations much higher than those he experienced at Bolton, Allardyce may yet discover that taking over at Newcastle is the footballing equivalent of the poisoned chalice. Much will depend on the start of the season: kick-off with a few good results and a top-half finish is possible; start badly and the pressure will build again.

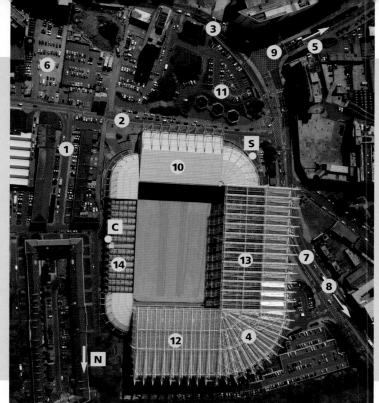

C Club Offices
S Club Shop

1 St. James's Park
2 Strawberry Place
3 Gallowgate
4 Away Section
5 To Newcastle Central BR
   Station (½ mile) &
   A6127(M)
6 Car Park
7 Barrack Road (A189)
8 To A1 and North
9 Corporation Street
10 Gallowgate End
11 Metro Station
12 Sir John Hall Stand
13 Millburn Stand
14 East Stand

↘ North direction (approx)

◀ 700356
▼ 700351

Northampton Town

Sixfields Stadium
Upton Way, Northampton, NN5 5QA

Tel No: 0870 822 1997

Advance Tickets Tel No: 0870 822 1966

Fax: 01604 751613

Web Site: www.ntfc.premiumtv.co.uk

E-Mail: normanhowells@ntfc.tv

League: League Two

Last Season: 14th
(P 15; W 14; D 17; L 7; GF 48; GA 51)

Training Ground: No specific facility

Nickname: The Cobblers

Brief History: Founded 1897. Former, County, Ground was part of Northamptonshire County Cricket Ground. Moved to Sixfields Stadium during early 1994/95 season. Record attendance 24,523 (at County Ground); 7,557 (at Sixfields)

(Total) Current Capacity: 7,653 (all seated)

Visiting Supporters' Allocation: 850 (in South Stand; can be increased to 1,150 if necessary)

Club Colours: Claret with white sleeved shirts, white shorts

Nearest Railway Station: Northampton

Parking (Car): Adjacent to Ground

Parking (Coach/Bus): Adjacent to Ground

Police Force and Tel No: Northants (01604 700700)

Disabled Visitors' Facilities:
Wheelchairs: Available on all four sides
Blind: Available

Anticipated Development(s): The club has plans to increase the capacity of the Sixfields stadium to c16,000 all-seated although there is no timescale for this work.

Appointed during the close season, following Colin Calderwood's defection to Nottingham Forest, John Gorman's reign at the Sixfields Stadium lasted barely six months as he resigned, for personal reasons, following the Cobblers defeat against Leyton Orient in December. The defeat left the team in 18th position, just above the League One drop zone. In early January the club announced that ex-Southampton boss Stuart Gray would be the new manager. Under Gray, the club's playing fortunes improved and the team gradually pulled away from the danger zone, ultimately finishing in a position of mid-table safety. Not all was positive on the field, however as the team suffered an embarrassing 4-1 defeat away at struggling Barnet in the second round of the FA Cup. For 2007/08, having had a season of consolidation following promotion at the end of the 2005/06 season, the club should have the potential to achieve a top-half finish.

N

C Club Offices
S Club Shop
E Entrance(s) for visiting
  supporters
R Refreshment bars for
  visiting supporters
T Toilets for visiting
  supporters

1 South Stand (away)
2 Athletics Stand
3 Upton Way
4 Car parks
5 A45 towards A43
  (Towcester and A5)
6 To Weedon Road
7 To Town Centre and
  station
8 A45 to M1 (Jct 16)

↘ North direction (approx)

◂ 699879
▾ 699819

Norwich City

Carrow Road
Norwich, NR1 1JE

Tel No: 01603 760760

Advance Tickets Tel No: 0870 444 1902

Fax: 01603 613886

Web Site: www.canaries.premiumtv.co.uk

E-Mail: reception@ncfc-canaries.co.uk

League: League Championship

Last Season: 16th
(46; W 16; D 9; L 21; GF 56; GA 64)

Training Ground: Colney Training Centre,
Hethersett Lane, Colney, Norwich NR4 7TS

Nickname: The Canaries

Brief History: Founded 1902. Former grounds:
Newmarket Road and the Nest, Rosary Road;
moved to Carrow Road in 1935. Founder-
members 3rd Division (1920). Record
attendance 43,984

(Total) Current Capacity: 26,034

Visiting Supporters' Allocation: 2,500
maximum in South Stand

Club Colours: Yellow with green side panel
shirts, green shorts

Nearest Railway Station: Norwich

Parking (Car): City centre car parks

Parking (Coach/Bus): Lower Clarence Road

Police Force and Tel No: Norfolk (01603 768769)

Disabled Visitors' Facilities:
Wheelchairs: New facility in corner infill
stand
Blind: Commentary available

Anticipated Development(s): The £3 million
corner infill between the new Jarrold (South)
Stand and the River End was opened in two
stages in early 2005. The upper tier provides
seats for 850 and the lower for 660. There is
also a new disabled area located between
the two tiers. This work takes Carrow Road's
capacity to 26,000. As part of the plans for
the Jarrold Stand, the pitch was relocated
one metre away from the City Stand; this will
facilitate the construction of a second tier on
the City Stand in the future if required.

In early October, following a 4-1 defeat at Carrow
Road by high-flying Burnley, Nigel Worthington was
sacked after almost six years in charge of the Canaries.
Although the team had started the season reasonably
well, a run of poor results left City just two points
above the drop zone following the Burnley defeat.
Martin Hunter took over briefly as caretaker before
the club appointed Peter Grant, an ex-player who had
been assistant manager at West Ham, to the
permanent post later in the month. Under Grant, the
Canaries' position improved but not dramatically and
the team ended up in 16th place. Having been in the
Championship for two seasons following their
relegation at the end of the 2004/05 season, the club's
parachute payments have ceased and with better
funded teams being relegated, the gap at the top of
the Championship grows larger. The team should be
capable of a top-half finish but the Play-Offs may be
the best that the club can aim for.

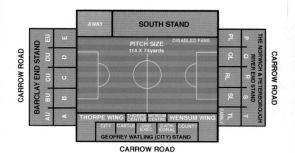

CARROW ROAD

C Club Offices
S Club Shop

1 Carrow Road
2 A47 King Street
3 River Wensum
4 Riverside
5 Car Park
6 To Norwich BR Station
7 South (Jarrold) Stand
8 Geoffrey Watling (City) Stand
9 Barclay End Stand
10 The Norwich & Peterborough (River End) Stand

↘ North direction (approx)

◄ 700795
▼ 700801

City Ground
Nottingham, NG2 5FJ

Tel No: 0115 982 4444

Advance Tickets Tel No: 0871 226 1980

Fax: 0115 982 4455

Web Site:
www.nottinghamforest.premiumtv.co.uk

E-Mail: enquiries@nottinghamforest.co.uk

League: League One

Last Season: 4th
(P46; W 23; D 13; L 10; GF 65; GA 41)

Training Ground: Nottingham Forest Football
Academy, Gresham Close, West Bridgford,
Nottingham NG2 7RQ

Nickname: The Reds

Brief History: Founded 1865 as Forest Football
Club, changed name to Nottingham Forest
(c1879). Former Grounds: Forest Recreation
Ground, Meadow Cricket Ground, Trent
Bridge (Cricket Ground), Parkside, Gregory
Ground and Town Ground, moved to City
Ground in 1898. Founder-members of Second
Division (1892). Record attendance 49,945

(Total) Current Capacity: 30,602 (all seated)

Visiting Supporters' Allocation: Approx 4,750

Club Colours: Red shirts, white shorts

Nearest Railway Station: Nottingham

Parking (Car): East car park and street parking

Parking (Coach/Bus): East car park

Police Force and Tel No: Nottinghamshire (0115
948 1888)

Disabled Visitors' Facilities:
Wheelchairs: Front of Brian Clough Stand
Blind: No special facility

Anticipated Development(s): In late June it was
announced that the club was planning a
possible relocation from the City Ground to a
new 50,000-seat ground at Clifton. If all goes
according to plan, the club anticipates moving
into the new £45-50 million ground for the
start of the 2014/15 season.

Under Colin Calderwood, Nottingham Forest's
second season in League One was as frustrating as
2005/06. For much of the season it looked again as
though Forest would achieve automatic promotion
and even on the final Saturday, the team was one of
three with a mathematical possibility of finishing
second behind champions Scunthorpe United. Apart
from Forest, Blackpool and Bristol City were also in the
frame. In the event, victories for both City and
Blackpool combined with Forest's home draw with
Crewe meant that Bristol was promoted and Forest,
with Blackpool, consigned to the Play-Offs. In the Play-
Offs, Forest faced Yeovil Town but defeat over the two
legs confirmed that Forest will again be playing in
League One in 2007/08. As before, Forest will
undoubtedly be one of the pre-season favourites for
automatic promotion and should certainly make the
Play-offs at the very least. Third time lucky, perhaps?

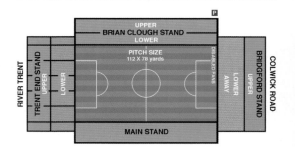

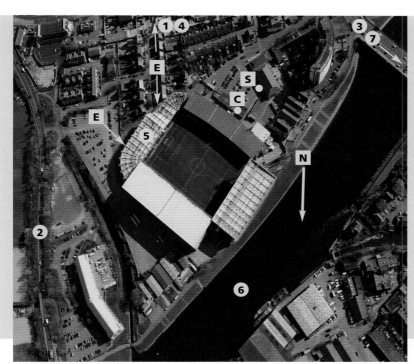

C Club Offices
S Club Shop
E Entrance(s) for visiting supporters

1 To Radcliffe Road
2 Lady Bay Bridge Road
3 Trent Bridge
4 To Trent Bridge Cricket Ground
5 Bridgford Stand
6 River Trent
7 To Nottingham Midland BR Station (½ mile)

↘ North direction (approx)

◀ 700807
▼ 700817

Notts County

Meadow Lane
Nottingham, NG2 3HJ

Tel No: 0115 952 9000

Advance Tickets Tel No: 0115 955 7204

Fax: 0115 955 3994

Web Site: www.nottscountyfc.premiumtv.co.uk

E-Mail: info@nottscountyfc.co.uk

League: League Two

Last Season: 13th
(P46; W 16; D 14; L 16; GF 55; GA 53)

Training Ground: Gedling Town FC, Riverside Ground, Stoke Lane, Stoke Bardolph, Nottingham NG14 5HX

Nickname: The Magpies

Brief History: Founded 1862 (oldest club in Football League) as Nottingham, changed to Notts County in c1882. Former Grounds: Notts Cricket Ground (Beeston), Castle Cricket Ground, Trent Bridge Cricket Ground, moved to Meadow Lane in 1910. Founder-members Football League (1888). Record attendance 47,310

(Total) Current Capacity: 20,300 (seated)

Visiting Supporters' Allocation: 5,438 (seated)

Club Colours: Black and white striped shirts, black shorts

Nearest Railway Station: Nottingham Midland

Parking (Car): Mainly street parking

Parking (Coach/Bus): Cattle market

Police Force and Tel No: Nottingham (0115 948 1888)

Disabled Visitors' Facilities:
Wheelchairs: Meadow Lane/Jimmy Sirrel/Derek Pavis Stands
Blind: No special facility

A much improved season at Meadow Lane saw Steve Thompson's side secure a position of mid-table safety after the near-miss of relegation at the end of the 2005/06 season. And the improved form was not limited to the league as the team achieved a couple of excellent away victories in the Carling Cup, beating Crystal Palace at Selhurst Park in the first round 2-1 before capping that with victory over Premier League Middlesbrough at the Riverside Stadium 2-0. For 2007/08, there is every possibility that progress on the field can be further maintained and a push for the Play-Offs is by no means an impossibility.

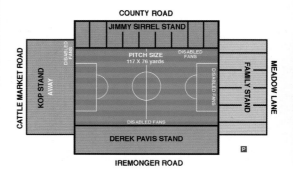

◀ 700818
▾ 700828

E Entrance(s) for visiting supporters
R Refreshment bars for visiting supporters
T Toilets for visiting supporters

1 A6011 Meadow Lane
2 County Road
3 A60 London Road
4 River Trent
5 Nottingham Midland BR Station (½ mile)
6 Jimmy Sirrel Stand
7 Kop Stand (away)
8 Derek Pavis Stand
9 Family (Meadow Lane) Stand

↘ North direction (approx)

Oldham Athletic

Boundary Park
Oldham, OL1 2PA

Tel No: 0871 226 2235

Advance Tickets Tel No: 0871 226 2235

Fax: 0871 226 1715

Web Site: www.oldhamathletic.premiumtv.co.uk

E-Mail: enquiries@oldhamathletic.co.uk

League: League One

Last Season: 6th
(P 46; W 21; D 12; L 13; GF 69; GA 47)

Training Ground: Chapel Road, Hollins, Oldham OL8 4QQ

Nickname: The Latics

Brief History: Founded 1897 as Pine Villa, changed name to Oldham Athletic in 1899. Former Grounds: Berry's Field, Pine Mill, Athletic Ground (later named Boundary Park), Hudson Fold, moved to Boundary Park in 1906. Record attendance 47,671

(Total) Current Capacity: 13,624 (all seated)

Visiting Supporters' Allocation: 1,800 minimum, 4,600 maximum

Club Colours: Blue shirts, blue shorts

Nearest Railway Station: Oldham Werneth

Parking (Car): Lookers Stand car park

Parking (Coach/Bus): At Ground

Other Clubs Sharing Ground: Oldham Roughyeads RLFC

Police Force and Tel No: Greater Manchester (0161 624 0444)

Disabled Visitors' Facilities:
Wheelchairs: Rochdale Road and Seton Stands
Blind: No special facility

Anticipated Development(s): Although the club originally had plans to relocate, it was announced in February that it was going to seek Planning Permission late in 2007 for the redevelopment of Boundary Park. The proposed £80 million plan would see three sides of the ground rebuilt with the intention of obtaining a 16,000 capacity. The redevelopment would also include a hotel, fitness club and offices. Other than the club awaits Planning Permission, there is no time scale for the work. It is likely that the first phase of the work will include the redevelopment of the existing Main Stand, with subsequent work including new stands on the south and west sides.

Under John Sheridan, Oldham had an improved season compared to 2005/06, when the team had just missed out on a Play-Off place. One of a number of teams vying for the Play-Offs during the 2006/07 season, ultimately Oldham's fate came down to the last Saturday of the season with two teams — Swansea and the Latics — vying for the all important sixth place. Both teams started the day with 72 points and a virtually identical goal difference; however, Oldham defeated relegated Chesterfield 1-0 at home whilst Swansea suffered a 6-3 home reverse against promotion chasing Blackpool. Oldham's victory set up a Play-Off semi-final against Blackpool. Unfortunately, the Lancashire side proved too strong, winning 2-1 at Boundary Park and 3-1 at Bloomfield Road. Thus Oldham face another season of League One football but confidence will be high that the team can, once again, make a serious challenge for the Play-Offs in 2007/08.

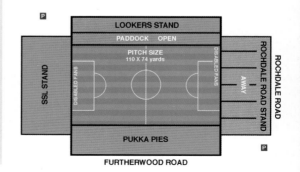

C Club Offices
E Entrance(s) for visiting
  supporters

1 A663 Broadway
2 Furtherwood Road
3 Chadderton Way
4 To A627(M) and M62
5 To Oldham Werneth BR
  Station (1½ miles)
6 Car Park
7 Rochdale Road Stand
  (away)
8 SSL Stand
9 Lookers Stand
10 Pukka Pies Stand

North direction (approx)

◄ 700830
▼ 700840

Peterborough United

London Road
Peterborough, Cambs, PE2 8AL

Tel No: 01733 563947

Advance Tickets Tel No: 01733 865674

Fax: 01733 344140

Web Site: www.theposh.premiumtv.co.uk

E-Mail: info@theposh.com

League: League Two

Last Season: 10th
(P 46; W 18; D11; L 17; GF 70; GA 61)

Training Ground: New facility being sought for the 2007/08 season

Nickname: Posh

Brief History: Founded in 1934 (no connection with former 'Peterborough and Fletton United' FC). Elected to Football League in 1960. Record attendance 30,096.

(Total) Current Capacity: 15,314 (7,669 seated)

Visiting Supporters' Allocation: 4,758 (756 seated)

Club Colours: Blue shirts, white shorts

Nearest Railway Station: Peterborough

Parking (Car): Peterborough

Parking (Coach/Bus): At ground

Police Force and Tel No: Cambridgeshire (01733 563232)

Disabled Visitors' Facilities:
Wheelchairs: South Stand
Blind: No special facility

Future Development(s): The club announced in mid-January that it was examining the possibility of seeking planning permission to replace the existing terraced Moys End Stand with a new 2,000-seat stand as part of a five-year plan that could ultimately see London Road converted into an all-seater stadium.

In mid-January, following a run of six straight defeats in the League, Keith Alexander departed as manager of United after a reign of less than eight months. The club, under the ownership now of Darragh MacAnthony (who acquired the club from Barry Fry), had started the season well but a slump in form saw the club drift lower in the League Two table and the defeat against Darlington was to cost Alexander his job. Assistant Coach Tommy Taylor was appointed as caretaker manager for a brief period before Darren Ferguson, son of Sir Alex, was made the new player-manager. Under the new boss, the club made significant progress on the field, ultimately reaching 10th place (albeit six points adrift of Shrewsbury in 7th place) although a challenge for a Play-Off place was undermined slightly by a run of only two wins in the club's last nine league matches. Provided that Ferguson can achieve more consistency and that the improvements can be sustained, then Posh should again be one of the teams challenging for a Play-Off place in 2007/08.

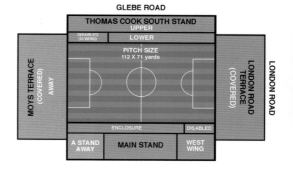

C Club Offices
S Club Shop
E Entrance(s) for visiting supporters
R Refreshment bars for visiting supporters
T Toilets for visiting supporters

1 A15 London Road
2 Car Parks
3 Peterborough BR Station (1 mile)
4 Glebe Road
5 A605
6 To A1 (north) (5 miles)
7 Main Stand
8 To Whittlesey
9 To A1 (south) (5 miles)
10 Thomas Cook Stand
11 London Road Terrace
12 Moys Terrace (away)

↘ North direction (approx)

◄ 700652
▾ 700662

Plymouth Argyle

Home Park
Plymouth, PL2 3DQ

Tel No: 01752 562561

Advance Tickets Tel No: 0845 388 7232

Fax: 01752 606167

Web-site: www.pafc.premiumtv.co.uk

E-mail: argyle@pafc.co.uk

League: League Championship

Last Season: 11th
(P 46; W 17; D 16; L 13; GF 63; GA 62)

Training Ground: Adjacent to ground

Brief History: Founded 1886 as Argyle Athletic Club, changed name to Plymouth Argyle in 1903. Founder-members Third Division (1920). Record attendance 43,596

(Total) Current Capacity: 19,500 (all seated)

Visiting Supporters' Allocation: 1,300 (all seated) in Barn Park End Stand up to maximum of 2,000

Club Colours: White and green shirts, green shorts

Nearest Railway Station: Plymouth

Parking (Car): Car park adjacent

Parking (Coach/Bus): Central car park

Police Force and Tel No: Devon & Cornwall (0990 777444)

Disabled Visitors' Facilities:
Wheelchairs: Devonport End
Blind: Commentary available

Anticipated Development(s): Work on the three new stands at Home Park progressed well, with work being completed during the 2001/02 season. Plans, however, for the demolition of the existing Main Stand and its replacement have been resurrected as part of a £37 million redevelopment to create a three-tiered structure taking the ground to 18,600 (all-seated). There is no confirmed timescale for this work.

Under Ian Holloway, Argyle had a much more successful season in 2006/07 than in the previous year when the team's scoring deficiencies had threatened the club's relegation. Whilst never one of the teams vying for automatic promotion or the Play-Offs, the Pilgrims finished in 11th Place eight points adrift of the all-important sixth place. However, with the three relegated teams looking fairly strong and with a number of other Championship teams — such as Southampton and Wolves — benefiting from the investment promised by new owners, it will be hard for teams such as Argyle to maintain a season-long challenge. Capable again of a top-half finish, the team may, however, find the Play-Offs a step too far.

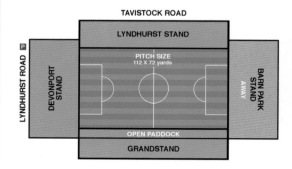

C Club Offices
S Club Shop

1 A386 Outland Road
2 Car Park
3 Devonport Road
4 Central Park
5 Town Centre & Plymouth BR Station (½ mile)
6 To A38 (½ mile)

North direction (approx)

◀ 692218
▾ 692209

Portsmouth

Fratton Park
57 Frogmore Road, Portsmouth, Hants, PO4 8RA

Tel No: 02392 731204

Advance Tickets Tel No: 0871 230 1898

Fax: 02392 734129

Web Site: www.pompeyfc.premiumtv.co.uk

E-Mail: info@pompeyfc.co.uk

League: F.A. Premier

Last Season: 9th
(P 38; W 14; D 12; L 12; GF 45; GA 42)

Training Ground: Stoneham Lane, Eastleigh
SO50 9HT

Nickname: Pompey

Brief History: Founded 1898. Founder-members
Third Division (1920). Record attendance
51,385

(Total) Current Capacity: 20,288 (all seated)
Visiting Supporters' Allocation: 3,121 (max)
in Milton Stand

Club Colours: Blue shirts, white shorts

Nearest Railway Station: Fratton

Parking (Car): Street parking

Parking (Coach/Bus): As directed by Police

Police Force and Tel No: Hampshire (02392
321111)

Disabled Visitors' Facilities:
Wheelchairs: TY Europe Stand
Blind: No special facility

Anticipated Development(s): In late April,
following take-over of the club by Alexandre
Gaydamak, the club announced plans to
relocate to a new 36,000-seat ground to be
constructed on reclaimed land in the city's
docklands area. The original plans for the
rebuilding of Fratton Park have, therefore
been abandoned and, following relocation,
the old ground will be redeveloped for
housing. It is intended that the club will seek
planning permission later in 2007 with the
intention of starting work in 2009 and
completion in 2011. As a temporary measure,
the club is applying for Planning Permission to
erect a roof over the open Milton Terrace.

ollowing the Great Escape at the end of 2005/06, Harry Redknapp's Portsmouth team started the 2006/07 season in similar vein, being one of the early season pacemakers. For Pompey fans, however, the promising start was not maintained and a gradual drift down the table ensured that the team was battling for a UEFA Cup spot rather than for the Champions League. In the event, however, even the UEFA Cup spots proved unachievable and the club ultimately finished in a respectable, but disappointing after the start, ninth place, two points off Bolton in seventh place. With considerable financial backing now in place behind him, Redknapp can be expected to strengthen the squad significantly in the close season and again Pompey should be one of the teams pushing for a UEFA Cup spot in 2007/08.

FA CUP

winners

2008

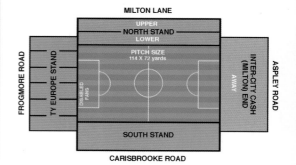

C Club Offices
S Club Shop
E Entrance(s) for visiting supporters
R Refreshment bars for visiting supporters
T Toilets for visiting supporters

1 Alverstone Road
2 Carisbrook Road
3 A288 Milton Road
4 A2030 Velder Avenue A27
5 A2030 Goldsmith Avenue
6 Fratton BR station (½ mile)
7 TY Europe Stand
8 Milton End
9 North Stand
10 South Stand

↘ North direction (approx)

◄ 699908
▼ 699898

Port Vale

Vale Park
Burslem, Stoke-on-Trent, ST6 1AW

Tel No: 01782 655800

Advance Tickets Tel No: 01782 655832

Fax: 01782 834981

Web Site: www.port-vale.premiumtv.co.uk

E-Mail: enquiries@port-vale.co.uk

League: League One

Last Season: 12th (P46; W 18; D 6; L 22; GF 64; GA 65)

Training Ground: Adjacent to ground

Nickname: The Valiants

Brief History: Founded 1876 as Burslem Port Vale, changed name to 'Port Vale' in 1907 (reformed club). Former Grounds: The Meadows Longport, Moorland Road Athletic Ground, Cobridge Athletic Grounds, Recreation Ground Hanley, moved to Vale Park in 1950. Founder-members Second Division (1892). Record attendance 49,768

(Total) Current Capacity: 23,000 (all seated)

Visiting Supporters' Allocation: 4,550 (in Hamil Road [Phones4U] Stand)

Club Colours: White shirts, black shorts

Nearest Railway Station: Longport (two miles)

Parking (Car): Car park at Ground

Parking (Coach/Bus): Hamil Road car park

Police Force and Tel No: Staffordshire (01782 577114)

Disabled Visitors' Facilities:
Wheelchairs: 20 spaces in new Britannic Disabled Stand
Blind: Commentary availaable

Anticipated Development(s): After some years of standing half completed, the club's new owners completed the roof over the Lorne Street Stand during the 2004/05 season. The Club is planning to instal seats in the remainder of the stand during the 2007/08 season.

Another season of mid-table mediocrity for Martin Foyle's team saw the Valiants improve one place on that achieved in 2005/06 to finish 12th in 2006/07 with a much better scoring record (although the improvement in scoring was countered by a much more porous defence as well — a total of 129 goals featured during the team's league campaign). The defensive problems were highlighted in an embarrassing 4-0 defeat away at League Two side Hereford United in the second round of the FA Cup. The Valiants look as though they are now established as a regular mid-table team in League One; however, as other teams have discovered, the division can be very tight and a couple of good or bad results can have a dramatic impact on a club's ultimate position.

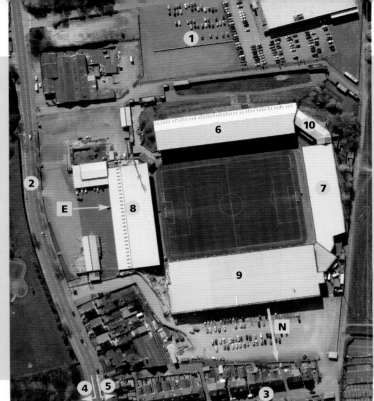

E Entrance(s) for visiting supporters

1 Car Parks
2 Hamil Road
3 Lorne Street
4 To B5051 Moorland Road
5 To Burslem Town Centre
6 Railway Stand
7 Sentinel Stand
8 Hamil Road Stand
9 Lorne Street Stand
10 Family Section

↘ North direction (approx)

◂ 700664
▾ 700669

Preston North End

Deepdale
Sir Tom Finney Way, Preston, PR1 6RU

Tel No: 0870 442 1964

Advance Tickets Tel No: 0870 4421966

Fax: 01772 693366

Web Site: www.pnefc.premiumtv.co.uk

E-Mail: enquiries@pne.com

League: League Championship

Last Season: 7th
(P 46; W 22; D 8; L 16; GF 64; GA 53)

Training Ground: Springfields Sports Ground, Dodney Drive, Lea, Preston PR2 1XR

Nickname: The Lilywhites

Brief History: Founded 1867 as a Rugby Club, changed to soccer in 1881. Former ground: Moor Park, moved to (later named) Deepdale in 1875. Founder-members Football League (1888). Record attendance 42,684

(Total) Current Capacity: 22,225 (all seated)

Visiting Supporters' Allocation: 6,000 maximum in Bill Shankly Stand

Club Colours: White shirts, blue shorts

Nearest Railway Station: Preston (2 miles)

Parking (Car): West Stand car park

Parking (Coach/Bus): West Stand car park

Police Force and Tel No: Lancashire (01772 203203)

Disabled Visitors' Facilities:
Wheelchairs: Tom Finney Stand and Bill Shankly Stand
Blind: Earphones Commentary

Anticipated Development(s): With three sides of the ground now rebuilt, the next phase of the redevelopment of Deepdale will involve the reconstruction of the Pavilion Stand. Current plans involve the construction of a single-tier stand accommodating 5,000 to take the ground's capacity to 24,000 although there is no confirmed timescale for this project as yet.

Under new manager Paul Simpson, North End again were serious challengers for a Play-Off place; unfortunately, however, unlike 2005/06 when the team finished in fourth place, in 2006/07, results on the final day conspired to leave Preston in seventh place a point behind Southampton but with a vastly inferior goal difference. In order to pip Southampton for the all important sixth place, Preston needed to better the result achieved by Saints. In the event, a 1-0 victory at home over promoted Birmingham City was not enough as Southampton defeated relegated Southend 4-1. Thus Simpson's team faces another season in the Championship and as the financial imbalance between the top teams in the Championship and those teams relegated from the Premier League gets ever wider it's hard to escape the view that the Play-Offs are again perhaps the best that North End fans can look forward to in 2007/08.

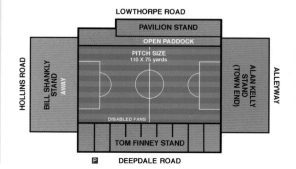

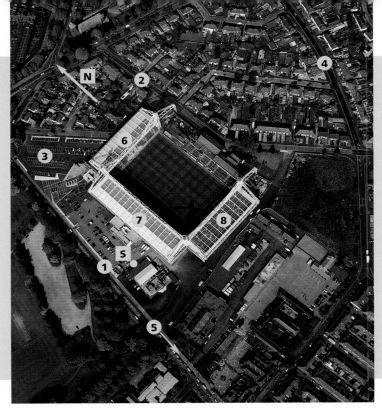

S Club Shop

1 A6033 Deepdale Road
2 Lawthorpe Road
3 Car Park
4 A5085 Blackpool Road
5 Preston BR Station
(2 miles)
6 Bill Shankly Stand
7 Tom Finney Stand
8 Town End Stand

↘ North direction (approx)

◂ 699138
▾ 699139

Loftus Road Stadium
South Africa Road, London, W12 7PA

Tel No: 020 8743 0262

Advance Tickets Tel No: 0870 112 1967

Fax: 020 8749 0994

Web Site: www.qpr.premiumtv.co.uk

E-Mail: boxoffice@qpr.co.uk

League: League Championship

Last Season: 21st
(P46; W 12; D 14; L 20; GF 50; GA 65)

Training Ground: Imperial College Sports Ground, Sipson Lane, Harlington, Middlesex UB3 5AQ

Nickname: The Superhoops

Brief History: Founded 1885 as 'St. Jude's Institute', amalgamated with Christchurch Rangers to become Queens Park Rangers in 1886. Football League record number of former Grounds and Ground moves (13 different venues, 17 changes), including White City Stadium (twice) final move to Loftus Road in 1963. Founder-members Third Division (1920). Record attendance (at Loftus Road) 35,353

(Total) Current Capacity: 19,130 (all seated)

Visiting Supporters' Allocation: 2,500 (maximum)

Club Colours: Blue and white hooped shirts, white shorts

Nearest Railway Station: Shepherds Bush and White City (both tube)

Parking (Car): White City NCP and street parking

Parking (Coach/Bus): White City NCP

Police Force and Tel No: Metropolitan (020 8741 6212)

Disabled Visitors' Facilities:
Wheelchairs: Ellerslie Road Stand and West Paddock
Blind: Ellerslie Road Stand

Anticipated Development(s): There is vague talk of possible relocation, but nothing has been confirmed. Given the constrained site occupied by Loftus Road, it will be difficult to increase the existing ground's capacity.

In late September, following the team's 3-2 defeat at League One side Port Vale in the Carling Cup and with the team in 24th place in the Championship, Gary Waddock stood down as manager, to be replaced by the highly experienced John Gregory. Waddock, however, remained with the club as Gregory's assistant. Under Gregory, Rangers battled strongly to ensure that they survived in the Championship, although it was touch and go right until the end with any one of four or five teams, including QPR, facing the possibility of being sucked into the drop zone. In the event, Rangers' League Championship status was effectively assured before the end of the season, making the final game of the season — at home against Stoke City — less significant than it might have been. Provided that the form shown in the second half of the season is replicated in 2007/08 then Rangers should be capable of a top half finish although it's unlikely that the team can achieve a top six finish.

C Club Offices
S Club Shop
E Entrance(s) for visiting
supporters

1 South Africa Road
2 To White City Tube
Station, A219 Wood Lane
and A40 Western Avenue
3 A4020 Uxbridge Road
4 To Shepherds Bush Tube
Station
5 To Acton Central Station
6 BBC Television Centre
7 Loftus Road
8 Bloemfontein Road

↘ North direction (approx)

◄ 700895
▼ 700889

Reading

Madejeski stadium
Bennet Road, Reading, RG2 0FL

Tel No: 0118 968 1100
Advance Tickets Tel No: 0870 999 1871
Fax: 0118 968 1101
Web Site: www.readingfc.premiumtv.co.uk
E-Mail: customerservice@readingfc.co.uk
League: F.A. Premier
Last Season: 8th
(P 38; W 16; D 7; L 15; GF 52; GA 47)
Training Ground: Reading FC Academy Training Ground, Hogwood Lane, Arborfield Garrison, Wokingham RG40 4QW
Nickname: The Royals
Brief History: Founded 1871. Amalgamated with Reading Hornets in 1877 and with Earley in 1889. Former Grounds: Reading Recreation Ground, Reading Cricket Ground, Coley Park, Caversham Cricket Cround and Elm Park (1895-1998); moved to the Madejski Stadium at the start of the 1998/99 season. Founder-members of the Third Division in 1920. Record attendance (at Elm Park) 33,042; (at Madejski Stadium) 24,122
(Total) Current Capacity: 24,200 (all seated)
Visiting Supporters' Allocation: 4,500 (maximum in the Fosters Lager South Stand)
Club Colours: White with blue hoops shirts, white shorts
Nearest Railway Station: Reading (2.5 miles)
Parking (Car): 1,800-space car park at the ground, 700 of these spaces are reserved
Parking (Coach/Bus): As directed
Other Clubs Sharing Ground: London Irish RUFC
Police Force and Tel No: Thames Valley (0118 953 6000)
Disabled Visitors' Facilities:
Wheelchairs: 128 designated spaces on all four sides of the ground
Blind: 12 places for match day commentaries
Anticipated Development(s): The club applied for Planning Permission to expand the capacity of the Madejski Stadium by 14,000 seats in October 2005, taking the ground's capacity up from 24,000 to 38,000. Permission was subsequently granted and will involve extending the North, South and East stands. Work is scheduled to start in the summer of 2008 with an anticipated completion date of the end of 2009.

Just as Wigan proved the pundits wrong in 2005/06, so Reading proved to be the surprise package of the 2006/07 season with Steve Coppell's side finishing in a highly creditable eighth position. Indeed, such was the team's form for much of the season, that a top seven finish and a place in the UEFA Cup was a distinct possibility — it was only the club's failure to better Bolton Wanderer's last day result that ultimately cost Reading seventh place (both teams drew, Reading away at Blackburn, Bolton at home to Aston Villa). Coppell, however, made it clear that he would continue to regard Premier League status as all important and that he'd be tempted to play fringe players had the team qualified. For 2007/08, Coppell's target will again be Premier League safety; the lesson from Wigan in 2006/07 was that the second season can prove trickier and much will depend on how effective Coppell is in strengthening his squad. A number of influential players, such as Steve Sidwell, have departed and, with both Sunderland and Birmingham being promoted, the threat from the new arrivals in the Premier League looks more potent than usual. Reading should have the potential to secure the team's Premier League status but a position of mid-table security is perhaps the best to be expected.

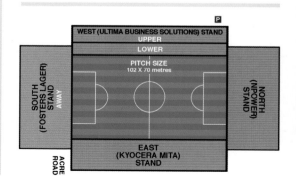

C Club Offices
S Club Shop

1 North Stand
2 East Stand
3 South Stand (away)
4 West Stand
5 A33 Basingstoke Road
6 A33 to M4 (Jct 11)
7 A33 to Reading Town Centre and station (two miles)
8 Hurst Way
9 Boot End

↘ North direction (approx)

◄ 699828
▼ 699833

Spotland Stadium
Willbutts Lane, Rochdale, OL11 5DS

Tel No: 0870 822 1907

Advance Tickets Tel No: 0870 822 1907

Fax: 01706 648466

Web-site: www.rochdaleafc.premiumtv.co.uk

E-Mail: info@rochdaleafc.co.uk

League: League Two

Last Season: 9th
(P46; W 18; D 12; L 16; GF 70; GA 50)

Training Ground: No specific facility

Nickname: The Dale

Brief History: Founded 1907 from former Rochadale Town F.C. (founded 1900). Founder-members Third Division North (1921). Record attendance 24,231

(Total) Current Capacity: 10,262 (8,342 seated) following completion of Pearl Street Stand

Visiting Supporters' Allocation: 3,650 (seated) in Willbutts Lane (Westrose Leisure) Stand

Club Colours: Blue shirts, blue shorts

Nearest Railway Station: Rochdale

Parking (Car): Rear of ground

Parking (Coach/Bus): Rear of ground

Other Clubs Sharing Ground: Rochdale Hornets RLFC

Police Force and Tel No: Greater Manchester (0161 872 5050)

Disabled Visitors' Facilities:
Wheelchairs: Main, WMG and Willbutts Lane stands – disabled area
Blind: Commentary available

Anticipated Development(s): None following completion of Willbutts Lane Stand.

After almost exactly three years into his second stint as boss at Spotland, Steve Parkin departed the managerial hot-seat in mid-December following a run of seven defeats in eight league games that left the team in 22nd place in League Two. Youth team manager Keith Hill took over as caretaker manager and, after a number of good results, was confirmed in the post until the end of the season. Under Hill's management Rochdale made steady progress up the League Two table, ultimately finishing in ninth position, some five points below Shrewsbury Town in the final Play-Off place. Dale's success was built around a good defence, with the club conceding only 50 league goals all season. For 2007/08, provided the team shows the type of form that it showed in the second half of 2006/07, then there is every possibility that the team will feature in the battle for the Play-Offs, although, as in 2006/07, it's likely that the automatic promotion places will be fought over by the teams relegated from League One.

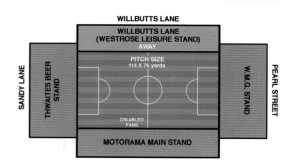

WILLBUTTS LANE

WILLBUTTS LANE
(WESTROSE LEISURE STAND)
AWAY

PITCH SIZE
114 X 76 yards

SANDY LANE

THWAITES BEER STAND

DISABLED FANS

W.M.G. STAND

PEARL STREET

MOTORAMA MAIN STAND

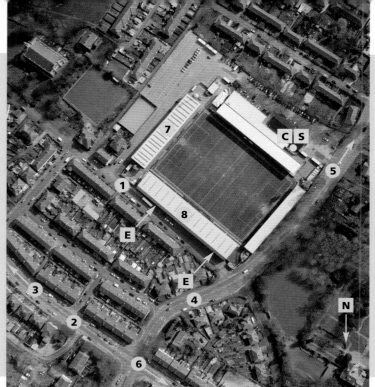

C Club Offices
S Club Shop
E Entrance(s) for visiting supporters

1 Willbutts Lane
2 A627 Edenfield Road
3 Rochdale BR Station (½ mile)
4 Sandy Lane
5 To M62
6 To M65 and North
7 Pearl Street (Westrose Leisure) Stand
8 Willbutts Lane Stand

N

↘ North direction (approx)

◀ 696966
▾ 696972

Rotherham United

Millmoor Ground
Millmoor Lane, Rotherham, S60 1HR

Tel No: 01709 512434

Advance Tickets Tel No: 0870 443 1884

Fax: 01709 512762

Web Site: www.themillers.premiumtv.co.uk

E-Mail: office@rotherhamunited.net

League: League Two

Last Season: 23rd (relegated; 10 points deducted for going into Administration)
(P 46; W 13; D 9; L 24; GF 58; GA 75)

Training Ground: Hooton Training Ground, Thomas Street, Kilnhurst, Mexborough S64 5TF

Nickname: The Millers

Brief History: Founded 1877 (as Thornhill later Thornhill United), changed name to Rotherham County in 1905 and to Rotherham United in 1925 (amalgamated with Rotherham Town – Football League members 1893-97 – in 1925). Former Grounds include: Red House Ground and Clifton Lane Cricket Ground, moved to Millmoor in 1907. Record attendance 25,170

(Total) Current Capacity: 7,500

Visiting Supporters' Allocation: 2,155 (all seated) in Railway End

Club Colours: Red shirts, white shorts

Nearest Railway Station: Rotherham Central

Parking (Car): Kimberworth and Main Street car parks, plus large car park adjacent to ground

Parking (Coach/Bus): As directed by Police

Police Force and Tel No: South Yorkshire (01709 371121)

Disabled Visitors' Facilities:
Wheelchairs: Millmoor Lane
Blind: Commentary available

Anticipated Developments(s): Despite the problems with the club's finances, which resulted in a 10 point penalty at the start of last season, work commenced on the construction of the new 4,200-seat Main Stand during 2006. The £3.3 million scheme was partially completed by the early part of the 2006/07 season.

Handed a 10-point penalty for going into Administration, the 2006/07 season was always going to be a struggle for United, but the campaign started reasonably well with the team, despite the penalty, looking as though a mid-table position was possible. However, a run of 14 games without a win saw the team drift to the bottom of the League One table and, on 12 March, manager Alan Knill, in charge at Millmoor since December 2005, was sacked. Mark Robins took over as caretaker with his position being made permanent just before Easter. Unfortunately, Robins wasn't able to arrest the team's gradual drift towards League Two and relegation was confirmed well before the end of the season. Moreover, such was the gap that the team would have been relegated even if the 10 points had not been deducted. As a relegated team, Rotherham would normally be considered to have the potential to make the Play-Offs at least but those teams relegated after Administration still face severe problems financially and the Millers may well struggle to sustain a serious push for promotion or the Play-Offs in 2007/08.

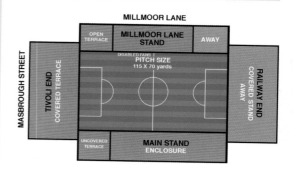

C Club Offices
S Club Shop
E Entrance(s) for visiting supporters
R Refreshment bars for visiting supporters
T Toilets for visiting supporters

1 Main Stand
2 To Rotherham Central BR Station
3 A6109 Masborough Street
4 Millmoor Lane
5 Station Road

↘ North direction (approx)

◄ 700688
▼ 700696

Scunthorpe United

Glanford Park,
Doncaster Road, Scunthorpe DN15 8TD

Tel No: 01724 848077

Advance Tickets Tel No: 0871 221 1899

Fax: 01724 857986

Web Site: www.scunthorpe-united.premiumtv.co.uk

E-mail: admin@scunthorpe-united.co.uk

League: League Championship

Last Season: 1st (promoted)
(P 46; W 26; D 13; L 7; GF 73; GA 35)

Training Ground: Grange Farm, Neap House Road, Gunness, Scunthorpe DN15 8TX

Nickname: The Iron

Brief History: Founded 1899 as Scunthorpe United, amalgamated with North Lindsey to become 'Scunthorpe & Lindsey United' in 1912. Changed name to Scunthorpe United in 1956. Former Grounds: Crosby (Lindsey United) and Old Showground, moved to Glanford Park in 1988. Elected to Football League in 1950. Record attendance 8,775 (23,935 at Old Showground)

(Total) Current Capacity: 9,200 (6,400 seated)

Visiting Supporters' Allocation: 1,678 (all seated) in South (Caparo Merchant Bar) Stand

Club Colours: Claret and blue shirts, claret shorts

Nearest Railway Station: Scunthorpe

Parking (Car): At ground

Parking (Coach/Bus): At ground

Police Force and Tel No: Humberside (01724 282888)

Disabled Visitors' Facilities:
Wheelchairs: County Chef Stand
Blind: Commentary available

Anticipated Development(s): Although a new stadium – Glanford Park opened in 1988 – there is a possibility that, in the future, the existing Evening Telegraph Stand will be demolished and replaced by a two-tier structure.

Although the Iron were challenging for automatic promotion at the time, Brian Laws resigned as manager in early November to take over at Sheffield Wednesday. He was replaced, on a caretaker basis, by Nigel Adkins. Under Adkins, United continued to make the running in League One and it came as no surprise that promotion was achieved well before the end of the season and that the League One title swiftly followed. Scunthorpe's success was based around a mean defence — the team only conceded 35 league goals all season — and a strong attack that scored some 73 goals during the season. This gave the Iron the greatest goal difference in the Football League. However, worryingly for the team, leading scorer Billy Sharp has indicated a desire to move on and the team will find that Championship attacks are more potent than those in League One. Away from the league, Scunthorpe suffered from the embarrassment of a home defeat, 2-0, by League Two strugglers Wrexham in the second round of the FA Cup. As a promoted team, Scunthorpe may well struggle in the Championship and 2007/08 could either see the team emulate Southend United and end in relegation or Barnsley and survive just.

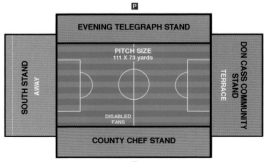

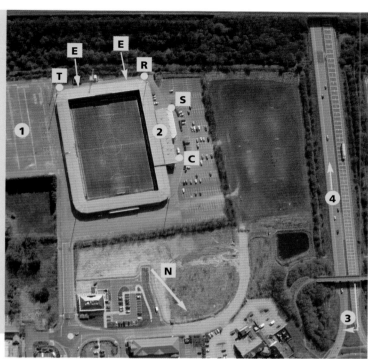

C Club Offices
S Club Shop
E Entrance(s) for visiting supporters
R Refreshment bars for visiting supporters
T Toilets for visiting supporters

1 Car Park
2 Evening Telegraph Stand
3 A18 to Scunthorpe BR Station and Town Centre (1½ miles)
4 M181 and M180 Junction 3

↘ North direction (approx)

◀ 700699
▼ 700707

Sheffield United

Bramall Lane
Sheffield, S2 4SU

Tel No: 0870 787 1960

Advance Tickets Tel No: 0870 787 1799

Fax: 0870 787 3345

Web Site: www.sufc.premiumtv.co.uk

E-Mail: info@sufc.co.uk

League: League Championship

Last Season: 18th (relegated)
(P 38; W 10; D 8; L 20; GF 32; GA 55)

Training Ground: The Hallam FM Academy @ Sheffield United, 614A Firshill Crescent, Sheffield S4 7DJ

Nickname: The Blades

Brief History: Founded 1889. (Sheffield Wednesday occasionally used Bramall Lane c1880.) Founder-members 2nd Division (1892). Record attendance 68,287

(Total) Current Capacity: 33,000 (all seated)

Visiting Supporters' Allocation: 2,700 (seated) can be increased to 5,200 if needed

Club Colours: Red and white striped shirts, black shorts

Nearest Railway Station: Sheffield Midland

Parking (Car): Street parking

Parking (Coach/Bus): As directed by Police

Police Force and Tel No: South Yorkshire (0114 276 8522)

Disabled Visitors' Facilities:
Wheelchairs: South Stand
Blind: Commentary available

Anticipated Development(s): Following the completion of the corner stand between the Bramall and Laver stands, which takes the ground's capacity to 33,000, the next phase in the development of Bramall Lane will be the reconstruction of the Hallam FM (Kop) Stand. This two-tiered structure is designed to add 4,000 seats to the ground's capacity. Planning Permission has also been granted for the construction of a 146-bedroom hotel behind the recently constructed corner stand.

Promoted to the Premier League at the end of 2006/07, the new campaign was always going to be a struggle for the Blades and the team's efforts to ensure Premier League survival were not assisted by the injury sustained by leading striker Rob Hulse. However, despite this loss, Neil Warnock's side battled hard to avoid the drop and it was only the last game of the season — against equally relegation threatened Wigan Athletic — that ultimately resulted in the Blades' relegation back to the Championship. The position is, however, more complicated than simply the number of points that the team gained during the season. There was considerable disquiet amongst a number of teams in the relegation zone over the failure to deduct points from West Ham United over the transfers of Mascherano and Tevez; whilst the Hammers were fined £5.5 million, there was no deduction of points and, given the importance of Tevez to the Hammers' ultimate survival, the other relegated teams believed that this was iniquitous. United, therefore, decided to take the Premier League's decision to appeal. Whilst this was going on, the waters got further muddied with the Premier League deciding to investigate the contract that saw Steve Kabba transferred from United to Watford. Away from the politics, the end of the season saw Warnock resign as manager; the club moved quickly to appoint Brian Robson to the hot-seat. As one of the teams relegated from the Premier League and with the benefit of the parachute payments, United will undoubtedly be one of the pre-season favourites to make an immediate return. Much will, however, depend upon how much of the existing squad Robson can retain and how well he is able to strengthen it.

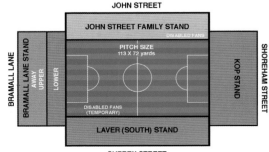

C Club Offices
S Club Shop
E Entrance(s) for visiting supporters

1 A621 Bramall Lane
2 Shoreham Street
3 Car Park
4 Sheffield Midland BR Station (¼ mile)
5 John Street
6 Hallam FM (Kop) Stand
7 John Street Stand
8 Bramall Lane (Gordon Lamb) Stand
9 Laver (South) Stand

↘ North direction (approx)

◄ 699964
▼ 699967

Sheffield Wednesday

Hillsborough
Sheffield, S6 1SW

Tel No: 0870 999 1867

Advance Tickets Tel No: 0870 999 1867

Fax: 0114 221 2122

Web Site: www.swfc.premiumtv.co.uk

E-Mail: enquiries@swfc.co.uk

League: League Championship

Last Season: 9th
(P 46; W 20; D 11; L 15; GF 70; GA 66)

Training Ground: Sheffield Wednesday Football Club Training Ground, Middlewood Road, Sheffield, S6 4HA

Nickname: The Owls

Brief History: Founded 1867 as The Wednesday F.C. (changed to Sheffield Wednesday c1930). Former Grounds: London Road, Wyrtle Road (Heeley), Sheaf House Ground, Encliffe & Olive Grove (Bramall Lane also used occasionally), moved to Hillsborough (then named 'Owlerton' in 1899). Founder-members Second Division (1892). Record attendance 72,841

(Total) Current Capacity: 39,859 (all seated)

Visiting Supporters' Allocation: 3,700 (all seated) in West Stand Upper

Club Colours: Blue and white striped shirts, black shorts

Nearest Railway Station: Sheffield (2 miles)

Parking (Car): Street Parking

Parking (Coach/Bus): Owlerton Stadium

Police Force and Tel No: South Yorkshire (0114 276 8522)

Disabled Visitors' Facilities:
Wheelchairs: North and Lower West Stands
Blind: Commentary available

Despite signing a brand-new contract tying Paul Sturrock to the club for a number of years early in the season, a poor run of form, culminating in a 4-0 drubbing at Championship new boys Colchester United (as a result of which the team had lost six out of 12 matches), the Owls sacked the Scotsman as manager towards the end of October. With Brian Laws, from Scunthorpe United, being appointed as full-time manager in early November. Under Laws, the team's form improved considerably and the team made steady progress up the League Championship table to such an extent that a Play-Off place was almost achieved. In the event, the final push towards a top-six berth proved a bit too much for the Owls, but finishing in ninth place, four points below Southampton in sixth place, indicates the considerable progress made under the astute management of Laws. Having had a successful second half to the 2006/07 season will increase confidence amongst the Wednesday faithful that in 2007/08 events at Hillsborough should be of more interest at the top rather than at the bottom of the table. With decent signings in the close season, Wednesday should have the potential to make a serious stab for the Play-Offs.

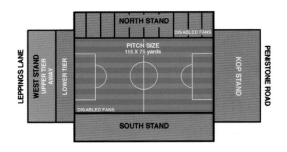

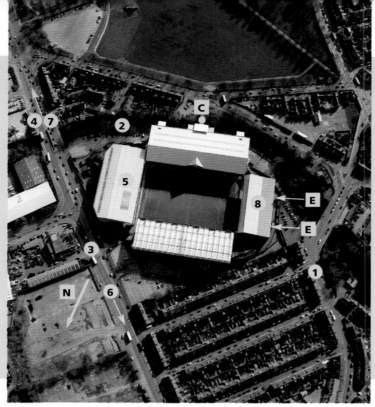

C Club Offices
E Entrance(s) for visiting supporters

1 Leppings Lane
2 River Don
3 A61 Penistone Road North
4 Sheffield BR Station and City Centre (2 miles)
5 Spion Kop
6 To M1 (North)
7 To M1 (South)
8 West Stand

↘ North direction (approx)

◄ 699978
▼ 699980

Shrewsbury Town

New Meadow
Shrewsbury, SY2 6QB

Telephone: 0173 360111*
Advance Tickets Tel No: 01743 360111*
Fax: 01743 236384*
* These are the numbers for the Gay Meadow and may not be transferred to the new ground.
Web Site: www.shrewsburytown.premiumtv.co.uk
E-mail: ian@shrewsburytown.co.uk
League: League Two
Last Season: 7th (P 46; W 18; D 17; L 11; GF 68; GA 46)
Training Ground: Sundorne Road, Shrewsbury SY1 4RQ
Nickname: The Shrews
Brief History: Founded 1886. Former Grounds: Monkmoor Racecourse, Ambler's Field; The Barracks Ground and the Gay Meadow (1910-2007); moved to the new ground for start of 2007/08 season. Elected to Football League 1950; relegated to Nationwide Conference at end of 2002/03 and promoted back to the Football league, via the Play-Offs, at the end of 2003/04. Record attendance at the Gay Meadow 18,917
(Total) Current Capacity: 10,000 (all-seated)
Visiting Supporters' Allocation: tbc (North Stand)
Club Colours: Blue shirts. Blue shorts
Nearest Railway Station: Shrewsbury (two miles)
Parking (Car): at ground
Parking (Coach/Bus): at ground
Police Force and Tel No: West Mercia (01743 232888)
Disabled Visitors' Facilities:
Wheelchairs:
Blind:
Anticipated Development(s): After a number of years, the Shrews finally achieved completion of the new ground for the start of the 2007/08 season.

The final season at the Gay Meadow for the Shrews was one of considerable success for Gary Peters and his team. As a result of a backlog of fixtures, the team's position in the League Two table was always slightly false and once the games-in-hand were played, the team's proximity to the Play-Offs became clear. However, it was not until the final tense Saturday of the season when three teams — Bristol Rovers, Shrewsbury and Stockport — were all in with a shout of the final two Play-Off places that the Shrews' destiny was decided. Bristol Rovers' 2-1 victory at Hartlepool combined with Town's 2-2 home draw against Grimsby meant that Stockport — 5-0 winners at Darlington — lost out. In the final game at the Gay Meadow, in the first leg of the Play-Off semi-final Milton Keynes Dons and Town drew 0-0. In the second leg at the National Hockey Stadium, Town came out on top 2-1 to set up a trip to Wembley to face Bristol Rovers. The final, however, was a game too far for the Shrews with Rovers ultimately winning 3-1. With the new ground to look forward to for the start of the 2007/08 season, there is considerable optimism that Town can build upon the success of 2006/07 and again aim for the Play-Offs at the very least.

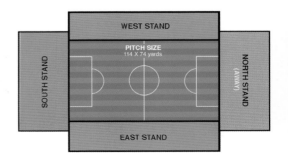

1 B4380 Oteley Road
2 Meole Brace roundabout
3 Shrewsbury-Hereford railway line
4 To Shrewsbury station (two miles)
5 A5112 Hereford Road to A5 (ring road)
6 A5191 Hereford Road to town centre and railway station
7 A5112 Hazledine Way

N

↘ North direction (approx)

◄ 700722
▼ 700721

Southampton

The Friends Provident St Mary's Stadium
Britannia Road, Southampton SO14 5FP

Tel No: 0845 688 9448

Advance Tickets Tel No: 0845 688 9288

Fax: 0845 688 9445

Web Site: www.saintsfc.co.uk

E-Mail: sfc@saintsfc.co.uk

League: League Championship

Last Season: 6th
(P46; W 21; D 12; L 13; GF 49; GA 50)

Training Ground: Staplewood, Club House, Long Lane, Marchwood, Southampton SO40 4WR

Nickname: The Saints

Brief History: Founded 1885 as 'Southampton St. Mary's Young Men's Association (changed name to Southampton in 1897). Former Grounds: Northlands Road, Antelope Ground, County Ground, moved to The Dell in 1898 and to St Mary's Stadium in 2001. Founder members Third Division (1920). Record attendance (at The Dell) 31,044 (at St Mary's) 32,151

(Total) Current Capacity: 32,689 (all-seated)

Visiting Supporters' Allocation: c3,200 in North Stand (can be increased to 4,750 if required)

Club Colours: Red and white shirts, black shorts

Nearest Railway Station: Southampton Central

Parking (Car): Street parking or town centre car parks

Parking (Coach/Bus): As directed by the police

Police Force and Tel No: Hampshire (02380 335444)

Disabled Visitors' Facilities:
Wheelchairs: c200 places
Blind: Commentary available

Anticipated Development(s): Following completion of the new stadium the club has no further plans at present.

One of a number of clubs to pass into foreign ownership, Southampton was taken over by an American during the course of the 2006/07 season. With the backing of the club's new owner, George Burley should be able to strengthen his squad during the close season and, if that's the case, then Saints should have the potential to improve on what ultimately proved to be a reasonably successful 2006/07 campaign. Never strong enough to be able to make a serious push for one of the two automatic promotion places, Saints did, however, achieve sixth place — but only just as Preston North End might have pipped them on the last day — and thus reach the Play-Offs. However, defeat by Derby County means that Championship football will again be on offer at St Mary's in 2007/08.

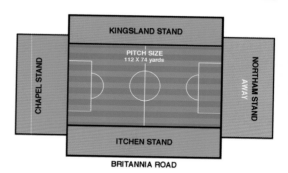

C Club Offices
S Club Shop
E Entrance(s) for visiting
supporters

1 A3024 Northam Road
2 B3028 Britannia Road
3 River Itchen
4 To M27 (five miles)
5 To Southampton Central
station and town centre
6 Marine Parade
7 To A3025 (and Itchen toll
bridge)
8 Belvedere Road
9 North Stand

↘ North direction (approx)

◄ 699202
▼ 699209

Southend United

Roots Hall Ground
Victoria Avenue, Southend-on-Sea, SS2 6NQ

Tel No: 01702 304050

Advance Tickets Tel No: 0844 477 0077

Fax: 01702 304124

Web Site:
www.southendunited.premiumtv.co.uk

E-mail: info@southend-united.co.uk

League: League One

Last Season: 22nd (relegated) (P46; W 10; D 12; L 24; GF 47; GA 70)

Training Ground: Eastern Avenue, Southend on Sea SS2 4DX

Nickname: The Shrimpers

Brief History: Founded 1906. Former Grounds: Roots Hall, Kursaal, the Stadium Grainger Road, moved to Roots Hall (new Ground) 1955. Founder-members Third Division (1920). Record attendance 31,033

(Total) Current Capacity: 12,392 (all seated)

Visiting Supporters' Allocation: 2,700 (maximum) (all seated) in North Stand and North West Enclosure

Club Colours: Blue shirts, blue shorts

Nearest Railway Station: Prittlewell

Parking (Car): Street parking

Parking (Coach/Bus): Car park at Ground

Police Force and Tel No: Essex (01702 431212)

Disabled Visitors' Facilities:
Wheelchairs: West Stand
Blind: Commentary available

Anticipated Development(s): The club submitted a proposal for the construction of its new £25 million 22,000-seat ground at Fossetts Farm to the council in early October and formal consent was granted by the council in January 2007 although this is now subject to a public inquiry. The new ground, designed by HOK (who also designed the Emirate Stadium), is scheduled for completion by the start of the 2008/09 season. A further complication is that planning permission for the redevelopment of Roots Hall is still outstanding.

Two promotions in two seasons meant that it was always going to be a struggle for Steve Tilson's Southend United team in the League Championship and so it proved for the Shrimpers with relegation back to League One being confirmed well before the end of the season. The team did not, however, go down without a fight and there were occasions when it looked as though the team might actually break free from the drop zone; in particular, league victory over Birmingham City away was particularly noteworthy. Another result of some considerable merit was a 1-0 triumph over Manchester United at Roots Hall in the fourth round of the Carling Cup. As a relegated team, Southend should have the potential to be challengers for a Play-Off place at the very least in 2007/08.

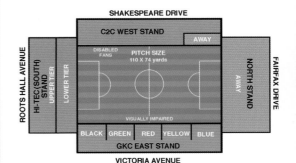

C Club Offices
E Entrance(s) for visiting supporters
R Refreshment bars for visiting supporters
T Toilets for visiting supporters

1 Director's Car Park
2 Prittlewell BR Station (¼ mile)
3 A127 Victoria Aveneue
4 Fairfax Drive
5 Southend centre (½ mile)
6 North (Universal Cycles) Stand

↘ North direction (approx)

◄ 697297
▼ 697286

Stockport County

Edgeley Park
Hardcastle Road, Edgeley, Stockport, SK3 9DD

Tel No: 0161 286 8888

Advance Tickets Tel No: 0161 286 8888

Fax: 0161 286 8900

Web Site:
www.stockportcounty.premiumtv.co.uk

E-Mail: fans@stockportcounty.com

League: League Two

Last Season: 8th
(P46; W 21; D 8; L 17; GF 65; GA 54)

Training Ground: Details omitted at club's request

Nickname: The Hatters

Brief History: Founded 1883 as Heaton Norris Rovers, changed name to Stockport County in 1890. Former Grounds: Heaton Norris Recreation Ground, Heaton Norris Wanderers Cricket Ground, Chorlton's Farm, Ash Inn Ground, Wilkes Field (Belmont Street) and Nursery Inn (Green Lane), moved to Edgeley Park in 1902. Record attendance 27,833

(Total) Current Capacity: 11,000 (all seated)

Visiting Supporters' Allocation: 800 (all seated) in Vernon Stand (can be increased by 1,500 all-seated on open Railway End if needed)

Club Colours: Blue with white stripe shirts, blue shorts

Nearest Railway Station: Stockport

Parking (Car): Street Parking

Parking (Coach/Bus): As directed by Police

Other Clubs Sharing Ground: Sale Sharks RUFC

Police Force and Tel No: Greater Manchester (0161 872 5050)

Disabled Visitors' Facilities:
Wheelchairs: Main and Cheadle stands
Blind: Headsets available

Anticipated Development(s): Although the club is still planning for the reconstruction of the Railway End, with the intention of constructing a new 5,500-seat capacity stand on the site, there is no time scale for this work (which had originally been planned for 1999/2000). Theoretically, the next phase after the Railway End would be an upgrade to the Vernon BS Stand, with the intention of making the ground's capacity 20,000.

Threatened with relegation at the end of the 2005/06 season, Jim Gannon's team had a much more successful campaign in 2006/07 and only just missed out on the Play-Offs following results on the last day of the season. Three teams — County, Shrewsbury Town and Bristol Rovers — were competing for the final two places. County had to win to ensure any chance whilst relying on either Bristol or Shrewsbury being defeated; in the event Bristol won just at champions Hartlepool whilst County trounced Darlington 5-0 away. However, Shrewsbury's nail-biting 2-2 draw at the Gay Meadow ensured that the Shropshire team held onto seventh place on goal difference. In 2006/07, the four relegated teams from League One dominated League Two; if the same happens in 2007/08 then the best that the Hatters can look forward to is the Play-Offs but the team should certainly have the potential to match or improve their performance in 2006/07.

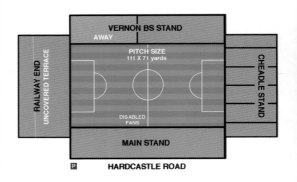

C Club Offices
E Entrance(s) for visiting supporters

1 Mercian Way
2 Hardcastle Road
3 Stockport BR station (¼ mile)
4 Railway End
5 Main Stand
6 Cheadle Stand
7 Vernon BS Stand

↘ North direction (approx)

◀ 695712
▼ 695706

Stoke City

Britannia Stadium
Stanley Matthews Way, Stoke-on-Trent ST4 4EG

Tel No: 01782 592222

Advance Tickets Tel No: 01782 592200

Fax: 01782 592221

Web Site: www.stokecityfc.premiumtv.co.uk

E-Mail: info@stokecityfc.com

League: League Championship

Last Season: 8th
(P46; W 19; D 16; L 11; GF 62; GA 41)

Training Ground: Michelin Sports Ground, Rose Tree Avenue, Trent Vale, Stoke On Trent, ST4 6NL

Nickname: The Potters

Brief History: Founded 1863 as Stoke F.C., amalgamated with Stoke Victoria in 1878, changed to Stoke City in 1925. Former Grounds: Sweetings Field, Victoria Ground (1878-1997), moved to new ground for start of 1997/98 season. Record attendance (at Victoria Ground): 51,380; at Britannia Stadium 28,218

(Total) Current Capacity: 28,383 (all-seater)

Visiting Supporters' Allocation: 4,800 (in the South Stand)

Club Colours: Red and white striped shirts, white shorts

Nearest Railway Station: Stoke-on-Trent

Parking (Car): The 650 parking spaces at the ground are for officials and guests only. The 1,600 spaces in the South car park are pre-booked only, with the majority held by season ticket holders. There is some on-street parking, but with a 10-15min walk.

Parking (Coach/Bus): As directed

Police Force and Tel No: Staffordshire (01782 744644)

Disabled Visitors' Facilities:
Wheelchairs: 164 places for disabled spectators
Blind: Commentaries available

Anticipated Development(s): There are long-term plans to increase the ground's to 30,000 by the construction of a corner stand between the John Smith Stand and the Boothen End but there is no timescale for this work.

Under Tony Pulis, restored to the team's management during the 2005/06 season, the Potters had a much improved season in 2006/07, ultimately finishing in eighth place and with the potential of achieving a Play-Off place not finally denied until the final match of the season. Three teams — Stoke, Southampton and Preston — were all capable of achieving the all-important sixth place. However, Stoke's 1-1 draw at Loftus Road with QPR combined with the Saints' 4-1 victory over Southend and Preston's 1-0 defeat of Birmingham City meant that Stoke missed out and that Championship football would again be on offer at the Britannia Stadium in 2007/08. With the number of well-funded teams vying for the top six places in the Championship increasing, City will do well to match their eighth position but should certainly feature in the pack chasing one of the Play-Off places.

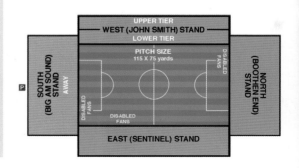

1 A50
2 To Stoke BR station
3 To A500 Queensway and
   City Centre, railway
   station and M6
4 North Stand
5 West Stand
6 East Stand
7 South Stand (away)
8 To Uttoxeter

↘ North direction (approx)

◄ 700729
▼ 700734

Sunderland

Stadium of Light
Sunderland, SR5 1SU

Tel No: 0191 551 5000

Advance Tickets Tel No: 0845 671 1973

Fax: 0191 551 5123

Web Site: www.safc.com

E-Mail: Via Website

League: F.A. Premier

Last Season: 1st (promoted)
(P 46; W 27; D 7; L 12; GF 76; GA 47)

Training Ground: The Academy Of Light,
Sunderland Road, Sunderland SR6 7UN

Nickname: Black Cats

Brief History: Founded 1879 as 'Sunderland &
District Teachers Association', changed to
'Sunderland Association' in 1880 and shortly
after to 'Sunderland'. Former Grounds: Blue
House Field, Groves Field (Ashbrooke), Horatio
Street, Abbs Field, Newcastle Road and Roker
Park (1898-1997); moved to Stadium of Light for
the start of the 1997/98 season. Record crowd (at
Roker Park): 75,118; at Stadium of Light (48,353)

(Total) Current Capacity: 49,000 all-seater

Visiting Supporters' Allocation: 3,000 (South
Stand)

Club Colours: Red and white striped shirts,
black shorts

Nearest Railway Station: Stadium of Light
(Tyne & Wear Metro)

Parking (Car): Car park at ground reserved for
season ticket holders. Limited on-street
parking (but the police may decide to
introduce restrictions). Otherwise off-street
parking in city centre

Parking (Coach/Bus): As directed

Police Force and Tel No: Tyne & Wear (0191 510
2020)

Disabled Visitors' Facilities:
Wheelchairs: 180 spots
Blind: Commentary available

Anticipated Development(s): The club has long
term plans to increase capacity at the Stadium
of Light by 7,200 in an expanded Metro FM
Stand and a further 9,000 in a second tier to the
McEwans Stand, taking the ultimate capacity of
the ground to 64,000. There is, however, no
confirmed. timescale and much will depend on
the club regaining — and retaining! — a place
in the Premier League.

The first managerial change of the season saw Niall
Quinn, whose consortium had taken over at
Sunderland in the close season following relegation at
the end of 2005/06, stand down as temporary boss at
the Stadium of Light following a disastrous start to the
campaign with the team having lost its opening four
games and having been dumped unceremoniously out
of the Carling Cup in the first round at League Two
strugglers Bury. It was announced towards the end of
August that Roy Keane, in his first managerial role,
would take over with the experienced Brian Kidd
being made assistant. Under Keane, Sunderland
prospered, making swift progress up the
Championship table and eventually competing with
Birmingham City and Derby County for the two
automatic promotion places. In the event Sunderland's
promotion was guaranteed before the 5-0 trouncing
of relegated Luton Town at Kenilworth Road,
although the victory did ensure that the title went to
Wearside. The last time that Sunderland reached the
Premier League, the club's one season proved to be
disastrous with relegation following immediately.
With Keane in charge and with a number of weaker
teams at the bottom end of the Premier League table,
the Black Cats should do considerably better in
2007/08.

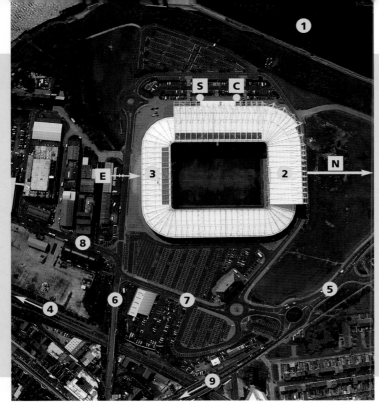

C Club Offices
S Club Shop
E Entrance(s) for visiting supporters

1 River Wear
2 North (McEwans) Stand
3 South (Metro FM) Stand (away)
4 To Sunderland BR station (0.5 mile)
5 Southwick Road
6 Stadium Way
7 Millennium Way
8 Hay Street
9 To Wearmouth Bridge (via A1018 North Bridge Street) to City Centre

North direction (approx)

699151
699159

Swansea City

Liberty Stadium
Morfa, Swansea, SA1 2FA

Telephone: 01792 616600
Advance Tickets Tel No: 0870 400004
Fax: 01792 616606
Web site: www.swanseacity.premiumtv.co.uk
E-mail: info@swanseacityfc.co.uk
League: League One
Last Season: 7th
  (P 46; W 20; D 12; L 14; GF 69; GA 53)
Training Ground: No specific facility
Nickname: The Swans
Brief History: Founded 1900 as Swansea Town, changed to Swansea City in 1970. Former grounds: various, including Recreation Ground, and Vetch Field (1912-2005); moved to the new ground for the start of the 2005/06 season. Founder-members Third Division (1920). Record attendance (at Vetch Field): 32,796; (at Liberty Stadium) 19,288.
(Total) Current Capacity: 20,500
Visiting Supporters' Allocation: 3,500 maximum in North Stand
Club Colours: white shirts, white shorts
Nearest Railway Station: Swansea
Parking (Car): Adjacent to ground
Parking (Coach/Bus): As directed
Other Clubs Sharing Ground: Swansea Ospreys RUFC
Police Force and Tel No: South Wales (01792 456999)
Disabled Visitors' Facilities:
Wheelchairs: tbc
Blind: tbc
Anticipated Development(s): After several years of uncertainty, Swansea City relocated to the new White Rock Stadium with its 20,000 all-seater capacity for the start of the 2005/06 season. The ground, which cost £27 million to construct and which was built near the site of the old Morfa stadium, is shared by the Swansea Ospreys RUFC team.

Despite a promising start to the season, which saw the Swans challenging initially for automatic promotion and then a place in the Play-Offs, a poor run in late January and early February, which saw the team drop out of the Play-Off positions coupled to criticism from both media and fans, led Kenny Jackett to leave the club on St Valentine's Day. He was replaced as caretaker-manager by Kevin Nugent. Towards the end of the month, the club appointed ex-midfielder Roberto Martinez, a Spaniard who had had three years with the Swans prior to a close season transfer to Chester City in 2006, on a two-year contract. Under Martinez, the Swans renewed their push for a Play-Off place with the team's ultimate fate not being decided until the final Saturday of the season. With both Oldham and Swansea vying for sixth place, the team with the better result would enter the Play-Offs although Athletic had a slightly better goal difference. In the event, goal difference was irrelevant as Oldham defeated Chesterfield at Boundary Park whilst the Swans crashed 6-3 at home to Play-Off bound Blackpool. Thus Swansea face a further season of League One football although the team should again be a serious candidate for both automatic promotion and the Play-Offs.

1 A4067 Ffordd Cwm Tawe Road
2 A4067 to A48 and M4 Junction 44 (five miles)
3 B4603 Neath Road
4 Brunel Way
5 Normandy Road
6 A4217
7 To Swansea city centre and BR railway station (two miles)
8 Parking
9 Cardiff-Swansea railway line

↘ North direction (approx)

◄ 700168
▼ 700180

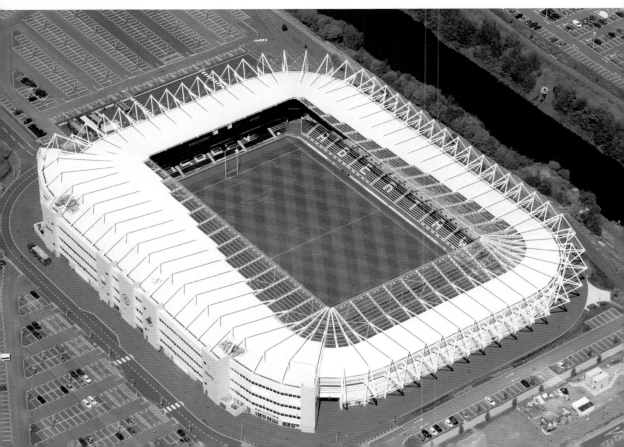

Swindon Town

County Ground
County Road, Swindon, SN1 2ED

Tel No: 0870 443 1969

Advance Tickets Tel No: 0870 443 1894

Fax: 01793 333703

Web Site:
www.swindontownfc.premiumtv.co.uk

E-Mail: enquiries@swindontownfc.co.uk

League: League One

Last Season: 3rd (promoted)
(P 46; W 25; D 10; L 11; GF 58; GA 38)

Training Ground: New facility being sought for the 2007/08 season

Nickname: The Robins

Brief History: Founded 1881. Former Grounds: Quarry Ground, Globe Road, Croft Ground, County Ground (adjacent to current Ground and now Cricket Ground), moved to current County Ground in 1896. Founder-members Third Division (1920). Record attendance 32,000

(Total) Current Capacity: 15,700 (all seated)

Visiting Supporters' Allocation: 3,342 (all seated) in Arkell's Stand and Stratton Bank (open)

Club Colours: Red shirts, white shorts

Nearest Railway Station: Swindon

Parking (Car): Town Centre

Parking (Coach/Bus): Adjacent car park

Police Force and Tel No: Wiltshire (01793 528111)

Disabled Visitors' Facilities:
Wheelchairs: In front of Arkell's Stand
Blind: Commentary available

Anticipated Development(s): The proposed relocation to the west of the town, at Shaw Tip, was thwarted in July 2004 when the local council decided not to sacrifice the community forest located at the site. The failure of the proposed move, which had been opposed by residents and many fans, resulted in the club seeking planning permission to redevelop its existing ground in February 2005. The club appointed a new director, Mike Bowden, in January and gave him special responsibility for the planned redevelopment of the County Ground.

Although appointed only during the summer and despite Town's reasonable progress in League Two, Dennis Wise departed in early November to take over as boss at Leeds United. The Robins moved quickly in appointing Wise's successor, with Paul Sturrock — recently sacked as manager of Sheffield Wednesday — taking over. In Sturrock's first game in charge, Swindon defeated League One outfit Carlisle United at the County Ground in the first round of the FA Cup — a good portent for the rest of the campaign. In the hunt for automatic promotion — along with the other three teams relegated at the end of the 2005/06 season, promotion back to League One was only guaranteed mathematically on the final day of the season when a 1-1 draw at home to promotion rivals Walsall meant that Milton Keynes Dons could not overtake them despite the Dons defeating Accrington Stanley 3-1. Sturrock has proved himself to be an astute manager at this level and he should be able to make a reasonable go of keeping Town in League One in 2007/08 although, as with any promoted team, sensible aspirations may be to see consolidation at least in the first season at this level.

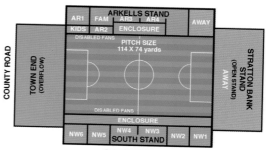

SHRIVENHAM ROAD

C Club Offices
S Club Shop
E Entrance(s) for visiting
supporters

1 Shrivenham Road
2 Stratton Bank (away)
3 A345 Queens Drive (M4
Junction 15 – 31/2 miles)
4 Swindon BR Station
(½ mile)
5 Town End
6 Car Park
7 County Cricket Ground
8 Nationwide Stand
9 Arkell's Stand
10 'Magic' Roundabout

↘ North direction (approx)

◂ 699231
▾ 699234

Tottenham Hotspur

White Hart Lane
Bill Nicholson Way, 748 High Road, Tottenham, London N17 0AP

Tel No: 0870 420 5000

Ticket Line: 0870 420 5000

Fax: 020 8365 5005

Web Site: www.tottenhamhotspur.com

E-Mail: email@tottenhamhotspur.com

League: F.A. Premier

Last Season: 5th
(P38; W 17; D 9; L 12; GF 57; GA 54)

Training Ground: Spurs Lodge, Luxborough Lane, Chigwell IG7 5AB

Nickname: Spurs

Brief History: Founded 1882 as 'Hotspur', changed name to Tottenham Hotspur in 1885. Former Grounds: Tottenham Marshes and Northumberland Park, moved to White Hart Lane in 1899. F.A. Cup winner 1901 (as a non-League club). Record attendance 75,038

(Total) Current Capacity: 36,257 (all seated)

Visiting Supporters' Allocation: 3,000 (in South and West Stands)

Club Colours: White shirts, navy blue shorts

Nearest Railway Station: White Hart Lane plus Seven Sisters and Manor House (tube)

Parking (Car): Street parking (min ¼ mile from ground)

Parking (Coach/Bus): Northumberland Park coach park

Police Force and Tel No: Metropolitan (0208 801 3443)

Disabled Visitors' Facilities:
Wheelchairs: North and South Stands (by prior arrangement)
Blind: Commentary available

Anticipated Development(s): Although the club was granted planning permission in October 2001 for the construction of a third tier on the East Stand, this project has not progressed and the club now seems to be turning its attention to a wholesale redevelopment of White Hart Lane to create a 50,000-seat ground. The work, if it progresses, will involve rotating the pitch 90° and Spurs groundsharing for a season whilst the work is completed.

Under Martin Jol, Spurs consolidated their position at the head of the pack chasing the top four, again finishing in fifth place — albeit eight points behind North London rivals Arsenal in the all-important fourth place — and thus again guaranteeing European football via the UEFA Cup in 2007/08. In 2006/07 Spurs had a good run in the UEFA Cup, losing ultimately to the holders Sevilla 4-3 on aggregate in the quarter-finals. Tottenham had lost 2-1 away in the first leg, but Sevilla scored twice in the first eight minutes at White Hart Lane to take an unassailable advantage, although Spurs did eventually draw the home tie 2-2. For Spurs, one of the close season captures, the Bulgarian Dimitar Berbatov, proved to be one of the signings of the season and with the squad being strengthened during the close season with the capture of the precocious Southampton teenager Gareth Bale and Darren Bent from relegated Charlton, there is every hope that in 2007/08 Spurs can capitalise on the uncertainties resulting from the departure of David Dein and Thierry Henry from the Gunners and perhaps make the breakthrough as serious challengers for a top-four spot.

C Club Offices
S Club Shop
E Entrance(s) for visiting
   supporters

1 Park Lane
2 A1010 High Road
3 White Hart Lane BR
   station
4 Paxton Road
5 Worcester Avenue
6 West Stand
7 South Stand

↘ North direction (approx)

◄ 700261
▼ 700254

Tranmere Rovers

Prenton Park
Prenton Road West, Birkenhead, CH42 9PY

Tel No: 0870 460 3333

Advance Tickets Tel No: 0870 460 3332

Fax: 0151 609 0606

Web Site:
www.tranmererovers.premiumtv.co.uk

E-Mail: info@tranmererovers.co.uk

League: League One

Last Season: 9th
(P46; W 18; D 13; L 15; GF 58; GA 53)

Training Ground: Raby Vale, Willaston Road,
Clatterbridge CH63 4JG

Nickname: Rovers

Brief History: Founded 1884 as Belmont F.C.,
changed name to Tranmere Rovers in 1885
(not connected to earlier 'Tranmere Rovers').
Former grounds: Steele's Field and
Ravenshaw's Field (also known as Old
Prenton Park, ground of Tranmere Rugby
Club), moved to (new) Prenton Park in 1911.
Founder-members 3rd Division North (1921).
Record attendance 24,424

(Total) Current Capacity: 16,587 (all seated)

Visiting Supporters' Allocation: 2,500 (all-
seated) in Cow Shed Stand

Club Colours: White shirts, white shorts

Nearest Railway Station: Hamilton Square or
Rock Ferry

Parking (Car): Car park at Ground

Parking (Coach/Bus): Car park at Ground

Police Force and Tel No: Merseyside (0151 709
6010)

Disabled Visitors' Facilities:
Wheelchairs: Main Stand
Blind: Commentary available

Under new manager Ronnie Moore, Rovers had a markedly better season in 2006/07 than in 2005/06 when, as the division's draw specialists, the team had been almost sucked into the relegation battle. In 2006/07, whilst never being strong enough to make a sustained challenge for a Play-Off place, a top half finish, only some eight points off the all-important sixth place, does offer a good foundation for a more sustained challenge in 2007/08. Not all was positive on the field, however, as League Two side Peterborough United came to Prenton Park in the second round of the FA Cup and won 2-1. Moore proved with Rotherham United that he could achieve promotion to League Championship level football and, with astute strengthening of the squad in the close season, Rovers might make a likely candidate to reach the Play-Offs.

C Club Offices
S Club Shop
E Entrance(s) for visiting supporters

1 Car Park
2 Prenton Road West
3 Borough Road
4 M53 Junction 4 (B5151) – 3 miles
5 Birkenhead (1 mile)
6 Cow Shed Stand
7 Kop Shed

↘ North direction (approx)

◀ 698977
▼ 698983

Walsall

Banks's Stadium
Bescot Crescent, Walsall, West Midlands, WS1 4SA

Tel No: 0870 442 0442

Advance Tickets Tel No: 0870 442 0111

Fax: 01922 613202

Web Site: www.saddlers.premiumtv.co.uk/

E-Mail: info@walsallfc.co.uk

League: League One

Last Season: 1st (promoted)
(P 46; W 25; D 14; L 7; GF 66; GA 34)

Training Ground: The Pavilion, Broad Lane, Essington, Wolverhampton WV11 2RH

Nickname: The Saddlers

Brief History: Founded 1888 as Walsall Town Swifts (amalgamation of Walsall Town – founded 1884 – and Walsall Swifts – founded 1885), changed name to Walsall in 1895. Former Grounds: The Chuckery, West Bromwich Road (twice), Hilary Street (later named Fellows Park, twice), moved to Bescot Stadium in 1990. Founder-members Second Division (1892). Record attendance 10,628 (25,343 at Fellows Park)

(Total) Current Capacity: 11,300 (all seated)

Visiting Supporters' Allocation: 2,000 maximum in William Sharp Stand

Club Colours: Red shirts, red shorts

Nearest Railway Station: Bescot

Parking (Car): Car park at Ground

Parking (Coach/Bus): Car park at Ground

Police Force and Tel No: West Midlands (01922 638111)

Disabled Visitors' Facilities:
Wheelchairs: Bank's Stand
Blind: No special facility

Anticipated Development(s): Planning permission was granted in the summer of 2004 for the redevelopment of the William Sharp Stand to add a further 2,300 seats, taking the away allocation up to 4,000 and the total ground capacity to 13,500. The project is to be funded via advertising directed towards the adjacent M6 but work has yet to commence.

Under Richard Money, the Saddlers, relegated at the end of the 2005/06 season, were always in the hunt for automatic promotion. In what turned out to be a four-team competition for the three automatic promotion spots from League Two, promotion was assured before the final game of the campaign with only the minor issue of the League Two title to be settled thereafter. Going into the final games of the season, the title could have been won by Hartlepool, Swindon or Walsall; in the event, Hartlepool's home defeat by Bristol Rovers combined with Walsall's away draw at Swindon meant that the silverware headed towards the Banks's Stadium. Although not a freescoring team, the Saddlers had one of the meanest defences in the Football League. Away from the league, Money's team also had some success in the Carling Cup, defeating League One outfit Plymouth Argyle 1-0 at Home Park in the first round. As a promoted team, the Saddlers' first priority will be to consolidate at the higher level, but the team has the potential to make a serious push for a good top half finish.

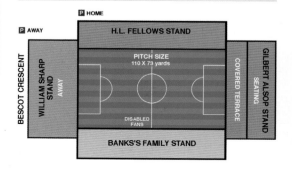

C Club Offices
S Club Shop
E Entrance(s) for visiting
   supporters

1 Motorway M6
2 M6 Junction 9
3 Bescot BR Station
4 Car Parks
5 Bescot Crescent
6 Gilbert Alsop Stand
7 William Sharp Stand

↘ North direction (approx)

◄ 699950
▼ 699960

Watford

Vicarage Road Stadium
Vicarage Road, Watford, WD18 0ER

Tel No: 0870 111 1881

Advance Tickets Tel No: 0870 111 1881

Fax: 01923 496001

Web Site: www.watfordfc.premiumtv.co.uk

E-Mail: yourvoice@watfordfc.com

League: League Championship

Last Season: 20th (relegated)
(P 38; W 5; D 13; L 20; GF 29; GA 59)

Training Ground: University College London Sports Grounds, Bell Lane, London Colney, St Albans AL2 1BZ

Nickname: The Hornets

Brief History: Founded 1898 as an amalgamation of West Herts (founded 1891) and Watford St. Mary's (founded early 1890s). Former Grounds: Wiggenhall Road (Watford St. Mary's) and West Herts Sports Ground, moved to Vicarage Road in 1922. Founder-members Third Division (1920). Record attendance 34,099

(Total) Current Capacity: 19,900 (all seated)

Visiting Supporters' Allocation: 4,500 maximum in Vicarage Road (North) Stand

Club Colours: Yellow shirts, red shorts

Nearest Railway Station: Watford High Street or Watford Junction

Parking (Car): Nearby multi-storey car park in town centre (10 mins walk)

Parking (Coach/Bus): Cardiff Road car park

Other Clubs Sharing Ground: Saracens RUFC

Police Force and Tel No: Hertfordshire (01923 472000)

Disabled Visitors' Facilities:
Wheelchairs: Corner East Stand and South Stand (special enclosure for approx. 24 wheelchairs), plus enclosure in North East Corner
Blind: Commentary available in the East Stand (20 seats, free of charge)

Anticipated Development(s): It was announced in September 2006 that the club intended to undertake a £32 million redevelopment of Vicarage Road in conjunction with the housing association Origin. The scheme will see the construction of a new East stand, taking the ground's capacity to almost 23,000.

Widely expected to be the Premier League's whipping boys in 2006/07, Adrian Boothroyd's team unfortunately fulfilled expectations and made an immediate return to the Championship after one season in the Premier League. The team's weakness throughout the season was the lack of up-front strength — the Hornets only scored 29 league goals all season — combined with a fairly leaky defence. Many games, however, were closely fought and, with a bit more luck, a few more victories might have resulted. Not having spent wildly, however, also means that the team is relegated in a reasonable financial position which, combined with the parachute payments, should mean that the team again challenges for both automatic promotion or the Play-Offs.

C Club Offices
S Club Shop

1 Vicarage Road
2 Occupation Road
3 Rous Stand
4 Town Centre (½ mile) –
Car Parks, High Street BR
Station
5 Vicarage Road Stand
(away)
6 East Stand
7 Rookery End

↘ North direction (approx)

◄ 699838
▼ 699842

West Bromwich Albion

The Hawthorns
Halfords Lane, West Bromwich, West Midlands, B71 4LF

Tel No: 0871 271 1100

Advance Tickets Tel No: 0871 271 9780

Fax: 0871 271 9861

Web Site: www.wba.premiumtv.co.uk

E-Mail: enquiries@wbafc.co.uk

League: League Championship

Last Season: 4th
(P 46; W 22; D 10; L 14; GF 81; GA 55)

Training Ground: Halfords Lane, West Bromwich B71 4LQ (the team also occasionally trains at the University of Aston ground at Great Barr)

Nickname: The Baggies

Brief History: Founded 1879. Former Grounds: Coopers Hill, Dartmouth Park, Four Acres, Stoney Lane, moved to the Hawthorns in 1900. Founder-members of Football League (1888). Record attendance 64,815

(Total) Current Capacity: 28,000 (all seated)

Visiting Supporters' Allocation: 3,000 in Smethwick End (can be increased to 5,200 if required)

Club Colours: Navy blue and white striped shirts, white shorts

Nearest Railway Station: The Hawthorns

Parking (Car): Halfords Lane and Rainbow Stand car parks

Parking (Coach/Bus): Rainbow Stand car park

Police Force and Tel No: West Midlands (0121 554 3414)

Disabled Visitors' Facilities:
Wheelchairs: Apollo 2000 and Smethwick Road End
Blind: Facility available

Anticipated Development(s): There is speculation that the club will seek to increase capacity to 30,000 by rebuilding the area between the Apollo and East stands, but nothing is confirmed.

Having been at The Hawthorns for almost two years, and having masterminded the club's escape at the end of the 2004/05 season only to see the team relegated at the end of 2005/06, Brian Robson departed the managerial hot-seat at West Brom following the team's 1-1 draw with Southend in mid-September. The result left the Baggies in ninth place. The club moved quickly to appoint Nigel Pearson as caretaker boss before confirming the appointment of ex-Hibernian manager Tony Mowbray to the full-time post in mid-October. Under Mowbray, the club made some progress on the field, although automatic promotion was beyond the team, ultimately finishing in fourth position and claiming a Play-Off place. Victory over the two legs against local rivals Wolverhampton Wanderers took the Baggies to Wembley to face Derby County for a place in the Premier League. Although West Brom had much of the play, it was County that scored the only goal with the result that Mowbray's team faces a second season back in the Championship. How well the team performs in 2007/08 will, to a considerable extent, depend on how many of his talented players Mowbray can keep — and already a number (such as Jason Koumas and Diomansy Kamara) look destined to depart. With strong teams coming down from the Premier League, it's going to get harder for a team like the Baggies to make a challenge for automatic promotion and so a Play-Off place is again perhaps the best that can be expected.

C Club Offices
S Club Shop
E Entrance(s) for visiting
   supporters

1 A41 Birmingham Road
2 To M5 Junction 1
3 Birmingham Centre
   (4 miles)
4 Halfords Lane
5 Main Stand
6 Smethwick End
7 Rolfe Street, Smethwick
   BR Station (1½ miles)
8 To The Hawthorns BR
   Station
9 East (Rainbow) Stand
10 Apollo 2000 Stand

↘ North direction (approx)

◄ 699262
▼ 699266

Boleyn Ground
Green Street, Upton Park, London, E13 9AZ

Tel No: 020 8548 2748

Advance Tickets Tel No: 0870 112 2700

Fax: 020 8548 2758

Web Site: www.whufc.co.uk

E-Mail: yourcomments@westhamunited.co.uk

League: F.A. Premier

Last Season: 15th
(P 38; W 12; D 5; L 21; GF 35; GA 59)

Training Ground: Chadwell Heath, Saville Road,
Romford RM6 6DT

Nickname: The Hammers

Brief History: Founded 1895 as Thames
Ironworks, changed name to West Ham
United in 1900. Former Grounds: Hermit
Road, Browning Road, The Memorial
Ground, moved to Boleyn Ground in 1904.
Record attendance 42,322

(Total) Current Capacity: 35,647 (all seated)

Visiting Supporters' Allocation: 3,700
maximum

Club Colours: Claret and blue shirts, white
shorts

Nearest Railway Station: Barking BR, Upton
Park (tube)

Parking (Car): Street parking

Parking (Coach/Bus): As directed by Police

Police Force and Tel No: Metropolitan (020
8593 8232)

Disabled Visitors' Facilities:
Wheelchairs: West Lower, Bobby Moore and
Centenary Stands
Blind: Commentaries available

Anticipated Development(s): The idea that
West Ham United might take over the 2012
Olympic Stadium was quashed in the spring of
2007. The club's new Icelandic owners have,
however, decided to examine the possibility of
relocation although nothing is confirmed at
this stage.

An eventful season for fans of the Hammers. Following the success in reaching the FA Cup final at the end of 2005/06, optimism was high at Upton Park that the team would further consolidate its position in the Premiership, although the arrival — in somewhat peculiar circumstances — of two Argentinian stars presaged a period of upheaval at the club that culminated in the team being acquired by an Icelandic consortium in November. Initially the new regime backed manager Alan Pardew, but, following a run of five defeats in six games culminating in a 4-0 defeat at Bolton that left the team deep in relegation trouble, Pardew was sacked in early December. The club moved quickly, with ex-Charlton manager (and Hammers' player) Alan Curbishley being appointed within days. Under Curbishley the club's form was variable — victories at home over Manchester United and away at Arsenal (the first defeat suffered by the Gunners at the new Emirates Stadium) but major defeats elsewhere — with the result that the club's Premier League status wasn't assured until the final Sunday of the season when a further unlikely victory — 1-0 over champions Manchester United at Old Trafford — combined with Sheffield United's defeat meant that the Yorkshire team was relegated. However, problems relating to the club's acquisition of the two Argentinian players led to the club being fined and a demand from other teams that the club be docked points — particularly as one of the two (Carlos Tevez) proved to be an inspirational factor in the club's ultimate survival.

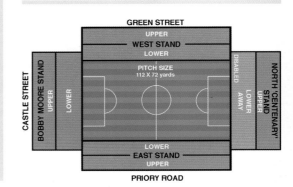

E Entrance(s) for visiting
supporters

1 A124 Barking Road
2 Green Street
3 North Stand
4 Upton Park Tube Station
  (¼ mile)
5 Barking BR Station (1
  mile)
6 Bobby Moore Stand
7 East Stand
8 West Stand

↘ North direction (approx)

◄ 699352
▼ 699342

Wigan Athletic

JJB Stadium
Robin Park Complex, Newtown, Wigan, Lancashire WN5 0UZ

Tel No: 01942 774000

Advance Tickets Tel No: 0871 663 3552

Fax: 01942 770477

Web Site: www.wiganlatics.premiumtv.co.uk

E-Mail: s.hayton@jjbstadium.co.uk

League: F.A. Premier

Last Season: 17th
(P 38; W 10; D 8; L 20; GF 37; GA 59)

Training Ground: Christopher Park, Wigan Lower Road, Standish Lower Ground, Wigan WN6 8LB

Nickname: The Latics

Brief History: Founded 1932. Springfield Park used by former Wigan Borough (Football League 1921-1931) but unrelated to current club. Elected to Football League in 1978 (the last club to be elected rather than promoted). Moved to JJB Stadium for start of 1999/2000 season. Record attendance at Springfield Park 27,500; at JJB Stadium 25,016

(Total) Current Capacity: 25,000 (all-seated)

Visiting Supporters' Allocation: 5,400 (maximum) in North Stand (all-seated)

Club Colours: White and blue shirts, blue shorts

Nearest Railway Stations: Wigan Wallgate/Wigan North Western (both about 1.5 miles away)

Parking (Car): 2,500 spaces at the ground

Parking (Coach/Bus): As directed

Other Clubs Sharing Ground: Wigan Warriors RLFC

Police Force and Tel No: Greater Manchester (0161 872 5050)

Disabled Visitors' Facilities:
Wheelchairs: 100 spaces
Blind: No special facility although it is hoped to have a system in place shortly

Anticipated Development(s): None following completion of the ground.

A difficult second season in the Premier League for Paul Jewel's Wigan team saw the club's fate not finally decided until the final match of the season. Although the Latics had been hovering over the drop zone for most of the season, the club entered the final game — a crunch match away at fellow strugglers Sheffield United where defeat for either team could lead to relegation — in 18th place. A tense match at Bramall Lane saw Wigan triumph 2-1 with the winning goal scored by ex-United player David Unsworth. An unlikely victory for West Ham United at Old Trafford led to Sheffield United being relegated. The following day, Jewel announced that he was resigning as manager in order to take a sabbatical and the club moved immediately to appoint assistant manager Chris Hutchings to the top job. This is not the first time that Hutchings has replaced Jewel as manager of a Premier League team and fans will be hoping that the previous experience — at Bradford City where he was boss for the first half of the season that led to the Bantams being relegated — will not be replicated at the JJB Stadium. With a number of potentially strong teams being promoted from the Championship, it could prove to be another hard battle to avoid the drop for Wigan.

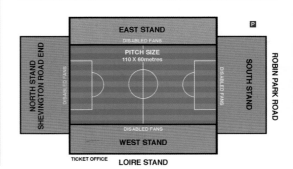

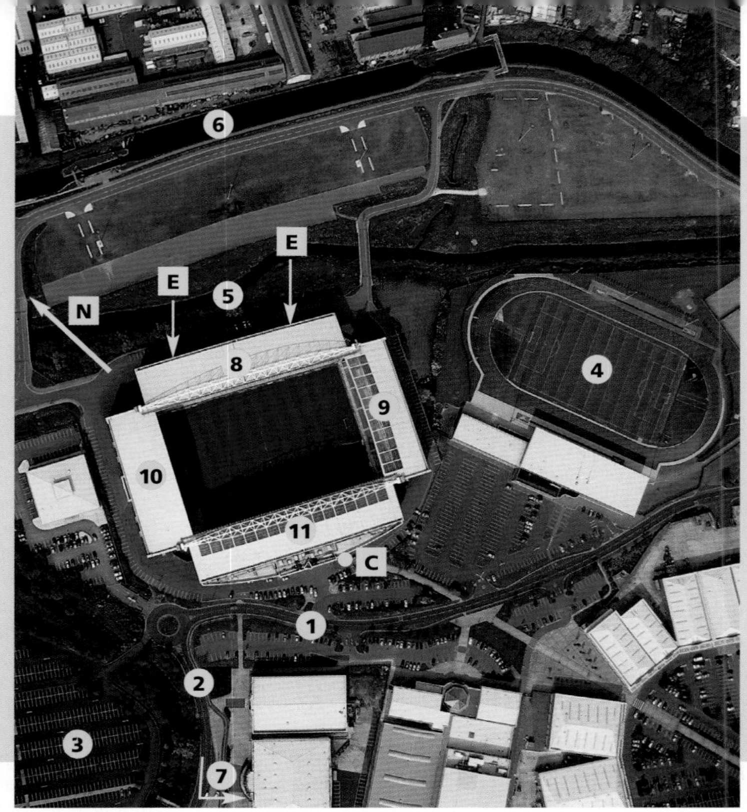

C Club Offices
E Entrance(s) for visiting supporters

1 Loire Drive
2 Anjoy Boulevard
3 Car Parks
4 Robin Park Arena
5 River Douglas
6 Leeds-Liverpool Canal
7 To A577/A49 and Wigan town centre plus Wigan (Wallgate) and Wigan (North Western) station
8 East Stand
9 South Stand
10 North Stand
11 West Stand

➘ North direction (approx)

◂ 699269
▾ 699272

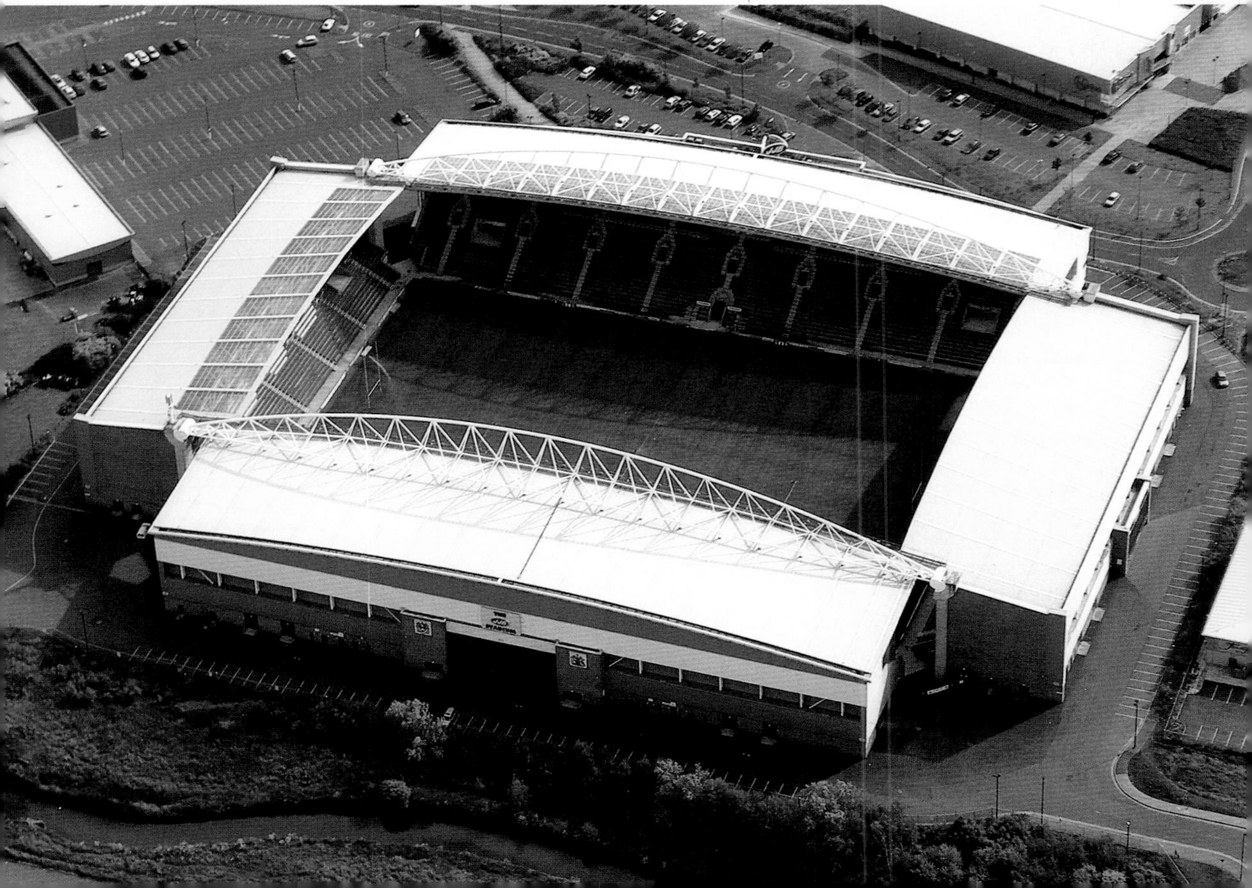

Molineux Ground
Waterloo Road, Wolverhampton, WV1 4QR

Tel No: 0870 442 0123

Advance Tickets Tel No: 0870 442 0123

Fax: 01902 687006

Web Site: www.wolves.premiumtv.co.uk

E-Mail: info@wolves.co.uk

League: League Championship

Last Season: 5th
(P 46; W 22; D 10; L 14; GF 59; GA 56)

Training Ground: The Sir Jack Hayward Training Ground, Douglas Turner Way, Wolverhampton WV3 9BF

Nickname: Wolves

Brief History: Founded 1877 as St. Lukes, combined with Goldthorn Hill to become Wolverhampton Wanderers in 1884. Former Grounds: Old Windmill Field, John Harper's Field and Dudley Road, moved to Molineux in 1889. Founder-members Football League (1888). Record attendance 61,315

(Total) Current Capacity: 28,500 (all seated)

Visiting Supporters' Allocation: 3,200 in lower tier of Steve Bull Stand or 2,000 in Jack Harris Stand

Club Colours: Gold shirts, black shorts

Nearest Railway Station: Wolverhampton

Parking (Car): West Park and adjacent North Bank

Parking (Coach/Bus): As directed by Police

Police Force and Tel No: West Midlands (01902 649000)

Disabled Visitors' Facilities:
Wheelchairs: 104 places on two sides
Blind: Commentary (by prior arrangement)

Anticipated Developments: The club installed some 900 seats on a temporary stand – now removed – between the Billy Wright and Jack Harris stands for the season in the Premiership. The club has plans to expand the capacity of Molineux to more than 40,000 by adding second tiers to the Stan Cullis and Jack Harris stands and completely rebuilding the Steve Bull Stand. There is no timescale for the work but it is unlikely to proceed until the club regains (and retains) a place in the Premiership.

A further season of some frustration for fans of Wolves saw the team achieve a Play-Off under Mick McCarthy — although this was only guaranteed on the last day of the season as a result of a 4-1 victory away at Leicester City as a number of other teams were also battling for the final two Play-Off places — only for the team to be defeated over the two legs by local rivals West Brom. Away from the league, Wolves suffered an embarrassing defeat, 6-5 on penalties, at home against League One strugglers Chesterfield in the first round of the Carling Cup. With the season completed it was announced that the club had been taken over by Steve Morgan, who had previously been interested in acquiring Liverpool. The deal that the new owner could buy the club for £10 provided that he ploughed some £30 million into developing the club. As a result, Wolves's financial position should improve immeasurably and McCarthy should be able to strengthen his squad accordingly. If that's the case then Wolves should certainly be a team to watch out for in 2007/08.

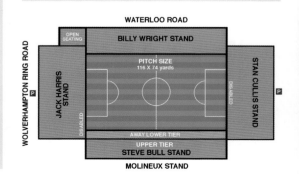

C Club Offices
S Club Shop
E Entrance(s) for visiting supporters
R Refreshment bars for visiting supporters
T Toilets for visiting supporters

1 Stan Cullis Stand
2 Steve Bull Stand
3 Billy Wright Stand
4 Ring Road – St. Peters
5 Waterloo Road
6 A449 Stafford Street
7 BR Station (½ mile)
8 Jack Harris Stand
9 Molineux Street
10 Molineux Way

↖ North direction (approx)

◄ 700864
▼ 700855

Racecourse Ground
Mold Road, Wrexham, Clwyd LL11 2AH

Tel No: 01978 262129

Advance Tickets Tel No: 01978 262129

Web Site: www.wrexhamafc.premiumtv.co.uk

E-Mail: geraint.parry@wrexhamfc.tv

Fax: 01978 357821

League: League Two

Last season: 19th
(P46; W 13; D 12; L 21; GF 43; 65)

Training Ground: Wrexham Football Club Centre Of Excellence, Colliers Park, Chester Road, Gresford, Wrexham LL12 8PW

Nickname: The Red Dragons or the Robins

Brief History: Founded 1873 (oldest Football Club in Wales). Former Ground: Acton Park, permanent move to Racecourse Ground c.1900. Founder-members Third Division North (1921). Record attendance 34,445

(Total) Current Capacity: 15,500 (10,500 seated)

Visiting Supporters' Allocation: 3,100 (maximum; all seated)

Club Colours: Red shirts, white shorts

Nearest Railway Station: Wrexham General

Parking (Car): (Nearby) Town car parks

Parking (Coach/Bus): As directed by Police

Police Force and Tel No: Wrexham Division (01978 290222)

Disabled Visitors' Facilities:
Wheelchairs: Pryce Griffiths Stand
Blind: No special facility

Anticipated Development(s): As part of the deal that saw the club move towards an exit from administration, the club announced in early June that it intended to redevelop the Crispin Lane (Kop) End of the ground. A new stand would be constructed along with flats and a 500sq m retail space. At the time of writing no formal permission for the work had been sought from the council nor was there a confirmed timescale for the work to be undertaken.

The first managerial casualty of 2007 was Denis Smith, whose reign at the Racecourse Ground had lasted since October 2001 and included some of the most turbulent events in the club's history, including the period in Administration that resulted in the club being the first to be docked 10 points under the new regulations. However, form on the pitch during the first half of the season resulted in the club languishing in 20th position, only two points off the drop zone. Smith and his assistant Kevin Russell were replaced by Brian Carey as caretaker and Joey Jones as coach. The new management team battled to keep Wrexham in the league although the club's fate was not finally determined until the final weekend of the season. Three clubs — Wrexham, Boston and Macclesfield — all faced the drop with the first two meeting at the Racecourse Ground with the knowledge that the team that lost would, in all probability, be playing in the Conference. It got even tighter for Wrexham as the visitors took a 1-0 lead. However, a strong comeback by the Red Dragons saw the team emerge victorious 3-1 and Boston consigned to the Conference. It was just as well that Wrexham won as Macclesfield's draw would have meant Wrexham Wrexham's relegation if the Welsh team had lost. Away from the league, the club did achieve one notable success in the FA Cup — a second round victory 2-0 over League One highfliers Scunthorpe United at Glanford Park. For 2007/08, with Carey confirmed as full-time boss, fans will be expecting an improvement in league form but perhaps a top half finish is the best that can be expected,

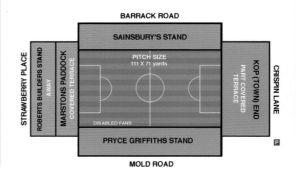

C Club Offices
S Club Shop
E Entrance(s) for visiting supporters
R Refreshment bars for visiting supporters
T Toilets for visiting supporters

1 Wrexham General Station
2 A541 – Mold Road
3 Wrexham Town Centre
4 Pryce Griffiths Stand
5 Kop Town End
6 To Wrexham Central Station
7 Roberts Builders Stand (away)

➘ North direction (approx)

◄ 700003
▼ 700007

Adams Park
Hillbottom Road, Sands, High Wycombe, Bucks HP12 4HJ

Tel No: 01494 472100

Advance Tickets Tel No: 01494 441118

Fax: 01494 527633

Web Site:
www.wycombewanderers.premiumtv.co.uk

E-Mail: wwfc@wwfc.com

League: League Two

Last season: 12th
(P46; W 16; D 14; L 16; GF 52; 47)

Training Ground: Marlow Road, Marlow
SL7 3DQ

Nickname: The Chairboys

Brief History: Founded 1884. Former Grounds:
The Rye, Spring Meadows, Loakes Park,
moved to Adams Park 1990. Promoted to
Football League 1993. Record attendance
15,678 (Loakes Park); 10,000 (Adams Park)

(Total) Current Capacity: 10,000 (8,250 seated)

Visiting Supporters' Allocation: c2,000 in the
Dreams (ex-Roger Vere) Stand

Club Colours: Sky blue with navy blue
quartered shirts, blue shorts

Nearest Railway Station: High Wycombe
(2½ miles)

Parking (Car): At Ground and Street parking

Parking (Coach/Bus): At Ground

Other Clubs Sharing Ground: London Wasps
RUFC

Police Force and Tel No: Thames Valley (01494
465888)

Disabled Visitors' Facilities:
Wheelchairs: Special shelter – Main Stand,
Hillbottom Road end
Blind: Commentary available

Anticipated Development(s): The club has
tentative plans to increase the ground's
capacity to some 12-15,000 through the
redevelopment of the Main Stand. There is,
however, no timescale for this work, a
project that would also require the
construction of a new access road.

Another season of some disappointment at Adams Park as Paul Lambert's team again threatened to make progress towards the Play-Offs only for form to drift and, ultimately, the club finished in a position of mid-table mediocrity. If league form was ultimately poor, the club did again have some success in the Carling Cup defeating League One side Swansea City 3-2 after extra time at the Liberty Stadium in the first round before triumphing 2-1 away at Premier League Fulham in the second round. A further victory in the quarter finals, 1-0 away at Premier League strugglers Charlton, took the Chairboys to their second semi-final in a cup competition in six years. However, the club was again to be defeated — this time by Chelsea. For 2007/08 the club should again have the potential to make the Play-Offs.

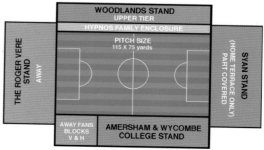

C Club Offices
S Club Shop
E Entrance(s) for visiting supporters

1 Car Park
2 Hillbottom Road (Industrial Estate)
3 M40 Junction 4 (approx 2 miles)
4 Wycombe Town Centre (approx 2½ miles)
5 Woodlands Stand
6 Roger Vere Stand (away)
7 Syan Stand
8 Amersham & Wycombe College Stand

➘ North direction (approx)

◀ 699217
▾ 699226

Yeovil

Huish Park
Huish Park, Lufton Way, Yeovil, Somerset BA22 8YF

Tel No: 01935 423662
Advance Tickets Tel No: 01935 423662
Fax: 01935 473956
Web Site: www.ytfc.premiumtv.co.uk
E-Mail: media@ytfc.net
League: League One
Last season: 5th
  (P46; W 23; D 10; L 13; GF 55; 39)
Training Ground: Huish Park (see above); the
  club has plans to relocate these facilities to
  Kingsbury Episcopi
Nickname: The Glovers
Brief History: Founded as Yeovil Casuals in 1895
  and merged with Petters United in 1920.
  Moved to old ground (Huish) in 1920 and
  relocated to Huish Park in 1990. Founder
  members of Alliance Premier League in 1979
  but relegated in 1985. Returned to Premier
  League in 1988 but again relegated in 1996.
  Promoted to the now retitled Conference in
  1997 and promoted to the Nationwide
  League in 2003. Record Attendance: (at
  Huish) 16,318 (at Huish Park) 9,348
(Total) Current Capacity: 9,400 (5,212 seated)
Visiting Supporters' Allocation: 1,700 on Copse
  Road Terrace (open) plus Limited seats in the
  Main Stand.
Club Colours: Green shirts, white shorts
Nearest Railway Station: Yeovil Junction or
  Yeovil Pen Mill
Parking (Car): Car park near to stadium for 800
  cars
Parking (Coach/Bus): As directed
Police Force and Tel No: Avon & Somerset
  (01935 415291)
Disabled Visitors' Facilities:
  Wheelchairs: Up to 20 dedicated located in
  the Bartlett Stand
  Blind: No special facility

Under Steve Thompson, Yeovil had a highly successful season in the club's second season in League One and, whilst never strong enough to be challenging for one of the automatic promotion places, a Play-Off place was ensured. In the Play-Offs, Yeovil faced Nottingham Forest — many people's favourite for automatic promotion — and winning 5-4 on aggregate — with the result that the Glovers ended up at Wembley where they faced Blackpool for the right to play in the League Championship. Unfortunately the final proved to be a match too far, with Blackpool running out 2-0 winners. The success of 2006/07 will, however, encourage belief that the team can make further progress in 2007/08. Not all of the season was positive, however; in the club's non-league days it was renowned as one of the great giant killers but in 2006/07 the boot was on the other foot as the team crashed out of the FA Cup in the first round as a result of a 3-1 defeat at Rushden & Diamonds of the Conference.

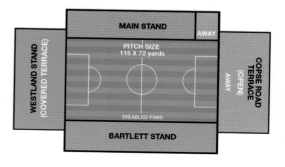

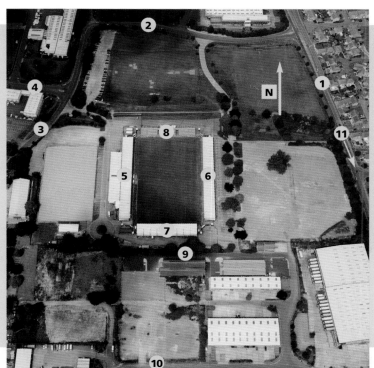

1 Western Avenue
2 Copse Road
3 Lufton Way
4 Artillery Road
5 Main (Yeovil College) Stand
6 Bartlett Stand
7 Westland Stand
8 Copse Road Terrace (away)
9 Memorial Road
10 Mead Avenue
11 To town centre (one mile) and stations (two to four miles)

↘ North direction (approx)

◀ 700937
▾ 700947

Millennium Stadium

Westgate Street, Cardiff CF10 1JA

Tel No: 0870 013 8600
Fax: 029 2023 2678
Stadium Tours: 029 208 22228
Web Site: www.millenniumstadium.com
E-Mail: info@cardiff-stadium.co.uk
Brief History: The stadium, built upon the site of the much-loved and historic Cardiff Arms Park, was opened in 2000 and cost in excess of £100 million (a tiny sum in comparison with the current forecast spend of over £600 million on the redevelopment of Wembley). As the national stadium for Wales, the ground will be primarily used in sporting terms by Rugby Union, but was used by the FA to host major fixtures (such as FA Cup and Carling Cup finals) until 2007 when the new Wembley was completed.
(Total) Current Capacity: 72,500
Nearest Railway Station: Cardiff Central
Parking (Car): Street parking only.

Parking (Coach/Bus): As directed by the police
Police Force and Tel No: South Wales (029 2022 2111)
Disabled Visitors' Facilities:
Wheelchairs: c250 designated seats. The whole stadium has been designed for ease of disabled access with lifts, etc.
Blind: Commentary available.
Anticipated Development(s): None planned

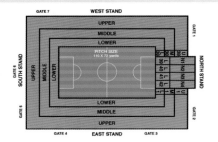